Our Ever Changing World:
Through the Eyes of Artists:

Artists, ART, & Story: A Moment in Time, 2020
International

Book 14

Foreword by Peter Clothier
Coordinated by Karrie Ross

*Our Ever Changing World: Through the Eyes of Artists ~ Book 14
Artist, ART, & Story: A Moment in Time 2020: International*
Foreword by Peter Clothier
Coordinated by Karrie Ross .

All rights reserved
Copyright © 2021 Karrie Ross

A Be-It-Now!™ Book

All rights reserved. No part of this book may be reproduced or transmitted in any form or by any means, electronic or mechanical, including photocopying, recording or by any other information storage and retrieval system, without written permission from the author/complier. Be It Now!™, are trademark. By buying and reading this book you agree to the following: NOTE: Disclaimer: Some of the observations may be X-rated. The ideas presented are based on the experience and contributions from participants and others, and do not reflect the publishers feelings. Your choice to read, consider or gain from the information is your own. This book is not for people who feel they need to blame others for their problems. And you take full responsibility for yourself and your mental, physical, emotional well-being. Any problems with the images or stories, please direct to the respective artist.The stories and images are ©copyright the artist/author and they take full responsibility to the truthfulness and attributing of people, places, things mentioned. Author, publisher, complier, organizer, is not to be held responsible for any miss-counting of events, or imagery, etc. understand that this is simply a set of opinions (and not advice) based on the experiences shared. You, the reader, are responsible for your own well-being, and hold Karrie Ross, the artists, and all members and affiliates harmless in any claim or event resulting from your reading, use, or application of the viewpoints shared in the book. I apologize for any mistakes I have made. I go through the book several times and double check as best possible, but I am human and mistakes happen. Please let me know and I will change it if I can. All rights to images and stories remain the rights of the respective artist.THIS BOOK IS NOT EDITED. WHAT IS WRITTEN IS FROM THE ARTISTS OWN WORDS.

Printed in the United States of America
Books are available for special promotions and premiums.
For details contact:
Published by Be It Now!, Los Angeles, CA 90247
email: info@beitnow.com
book website: http://www.artistartandstory.com

ISBN 13: 9798726083032

Book Design: www.KarrieRoss.com
ALL story and imagery is © per, respective artist and
all rights reserved by artist.

To all the Artists, who participated.
For sharing "that special feeling."
Thank you

The following are remembered:
(note some are from 2021)

Roger Morrison, July 25, 2020, Pasadena, CA

Roland Reiss, December 13, 2020, Los Angeles, CA

Chantal, February, 2020, Los Angeles, CA

Simone Gad, February 25, 2021, Los Angeles, CA

Liz Young, https://en.m.wikipedia.org/wiki/Liz_Young

Van Arno, 18/01/2021, Ventura, CA

Christopher Purvis Aka "Kiffy", April 7, 2020,
Mountain View CA

Mansoureh Kheyabani Homaie, March 5th, 2021, Tehran Iran

Paula A. Fiore, November 24, 2020, Wakefield, RI

Jackie Saccoccio, December 4, 2020, West Cornwall, CT

Kathy I. King, December 16, 2020, Santa Barbara, CA

My father, Peter Saccoccio, August 16, 2020, Johnston, RI

Stepmother-in-law, Karen E. Winick, September 26, 2020.
West Hartford, CT

Our Ever Changing World: Through the Eyes of Artists: Book 14

Other Books by Karrie Ross

—————————— BOOKs ——————————

The Big Little Book of Thoughts
My Breasts Talking; My Hands Talking; My Trees Talking

Got Shui?

Coaching Parent Coaching Child:
3x award winning self-help and Parenting book

The Bebuddies.com Books
Be Watchful: EnviroNate (*award winning book*)
Be Healthy: Doc ; Be Kind: CareyAngel

Books by BzzzBee the Bee
BZZZed ; You Have My Heart; SnowBee

Our Ever Changing World: Through the Eyes of Artists:

Book One:*	What are you Saving from Extinction? 2013
Book Two: *	Couples and Collaborations 2014
Book Four:	Artists ART & Story 2015
Book Five:	Idle Chatter: What's In Your Cupboard? 2015
Book Six:	Artists ART & Story: Best of 2016
Book Seven:	Artists ART & Story: A Moment in 2017: U.S.A.
Book Eight*:	Ann Marie Rouseau: The Women's March 2017
Book Nine:*	California: The High Desert Artists, 2018
Book Ten:	Artists ART & Story: A Moment in Time, 2018: International
Book Eleven:	Artists Art & Story: A Moment in Time, 2019
Book Twelve:*	#spareasquare: When TP became a rare commodity. 4/color; 2020
Book Thirteen*	EGGs: Coloring Book; 2020
Book Fourteen	Artists ART & Story: A Moment in Time, 2020: International

* 4/color book

FOREWORD

by Peter Clothier

2020: A Brief History

Seriously? 2020? Do we really need to revisit this annus maximus horribilis? (And wouldn't anus be more apt?) Still, for history's sake it behooves us to remember...

... that the year began inauspiciously with the mockery of a Senate "trial" in which Republican senators declined to hear so much as a single witness against a transparently narcissistic, cruel, corrupt, incompetent president whose name I choose not to honor with a mention.

Only shortly afterwards, we heard the first whisperings about the malignant virus that would soon spread into a deadly, world-wide pandemic. Here in the United States the president's mindless lies and embrace of quackery instead of sound medical science would lead to the death of more than a quarter million Americans—and the bleak certainty of many more to come.

Otherwise: the dire truth of long-ignored warnings about climate from the world's scientists defied further denial as the planet experienced record-setting wildfires in Australia, first, then on our own West Coast—disasters followed shortly by a never ending march of powerful hurricanes and cyclones East and West, and that rare, astonishing "derecho" that ravaged the Midwest.

This, too, was the year of George Floyd, a Black man whose very public murder by a police officer was recorded in horrifying detail, along a succession of all-too familiar murders of Black men and women at the hands of those sworn to protect and serve.

It was a year of bitter social and cultural animosity; of the white supremacist Proud Boys and Boogaloos parading in our streets with long guns; of terrorist threats against political leaders and the actual, hostile invasion of a State House; of arson and looting in American cities, while the occupant of our Oval Office took delight in adding gasoline to the flames.

It was, most sadly, the year in which the noble, feisty, righteously liberal Justice Ruth Bader Ginsberg finally succumbed to cancer; and—in defiance of her dying wish---of the unseemly rush to replace her with the embodiment of everything she was devoted to opposing.

It was a year of chaos and shameless corruption in government, a year in which elected US Senators chose spineless servility in the face of presidential self-service and grift.

And toward the end, in the course of and after the election, this was the year in which American politicians and officials stood by in fearful and permissive silence as the

Artist, ART, & Story: A Moment in Time, 2020: International

President of the United States, no less, subjected the country to weeks of despicable lies, false accusations and subterfuge in a desperate, infantile attempt to retore his ego and assert his power at the expense of the foundational principles of American democracy.

So ends the annus horribilis, 2020. And yet... and still... let's remember this: there was the resurgence of Black Lives Matter. There was a resounding and hopefully lasting recognition of the persistence of injustice in America—whether racial, religion- or gender-based, social or financial. 2020 helped us to reach an understanding, expressed in the electoral choices of American voters, that these are issues that must no longer be ignored or shelved if we are to pursue our national aspiration for that "more perfect union."

The silver lining of the gloom and the storm clouds of 2020 is to have activated a rebirth of social conscience and to have lit a fire in the hearts of millions of our citizens—young people, especially, women, people of color—with the determination to achieve a better 2021. This could prove to have been the year in which we humans saw the beginnings of a long-awaited paradigm shift in planetary consciousness.

****
PETER CLOTHIER continues to enjoy a multi-year recovery from an early academic career, writing mostly about art and artists since the early 1970s. Aside from countless articles and reviews in national magazines, he's the author of two books of poetry, three novels, a children's book, and David Hockney in the Abbeville Modern Masters

series. His essay collections, including Persist: In Praise of the Creative Spirit In a World Gone Mad With Commerce have found a receptive audience; and his blogs, including most notably The Buddha Diaries, attract an international readership. A long-time meditation practitioner, he is known for his popular "One Hour/One Painting" series, in sessions that merge the ancient skills of meditation and contemplation and foster the art of conscious looking.

INTRODUCTION

~ an introduction deals with the subject of the book, supplementing and introducing the text and indicating a point of view to be adopted by the reader. ~

I BELIEVE THAT ARTISTS ARE IN SOME WAY HISTORIANS…that their work saves something from becoming forgotten. And, artists tell stories all the time in their art, words, visuals. Moments.

The year 2020: A year seen as "a moment in time' all by itself, a year of unprecedented change. A moment that was aggravated by uncertainty, fear, and a paranoia not experienced in my lifetime.

> **mo·ment**
> /ˈmōmənt/ 🔊
> *noun*
> 1. a very brief period of time.
>   "she was silent for a moment before replying"
>   *synonyms:* little while, short time, bit, minute, second, instant, split second; More
> 2. FORMAL
>   importance.
>   "the issues were of little moment to the electorate"
>   *synonyms:* importance, import, significance, consequence, substance, note, mark, prominence, value, weight, concern, interest, gravity, seriousness
>   "the issues were of little moment to the voters"

I found it hard to begin the production on this book for many reasons. Several very special people to me, passed away. I would find that as I was reviewing the stories, that my eyes were bluring, tears were rolling down my cheeks and I would stop.

This years stories have a bit heavier social political comments, I view this as being the dark cloud that was over our heads. So much confusion and uncertainty, things that go along with change and that we had by the bucket-full in 2020.

As always, this is my art-book-project, entry is free and most submissions are accepted as long as they are on track with the focus of the book. I price the book just enough to make it into Amazons library system, and once on Amazon, books seldom get deleted...so these will live on as long as amazon.com does.

Thank you for being a part of this journey
Karrie Ross
instagram: @karrierossart
website: http://www.karrieross.com
book site: http://www.artistartandstory.com

Note: The artists are listed in the order if when they submitted their stories. I appologize if I left anyone out anywhere or misscoppied anything. The book has not been edited or proofed by me, so spelling, grammar and sentence structure is purely of the artists own words and adds to the quality of the sharing.

Thankful ...
I appreciate all the stories submitted, I really like to have a big book, and therefore even the stories a little off-track have been included. A big hug and many thanks especially to the Artists that kept to my requested focus of the year 2020.

Artist, ART, & Story: A Moment in Time, 2020: International

Artists

Listing of 48 Artists in Order of Appearance

Laura Larson 15	Stevie Love 121
Kerrie Smith 18	Kaz Maslanka 126
Jan Book 20	Doug Eisenstark 134
Sheila Fein 24	Hadiya Finley 139
Laurence de B Anderson .30	Lisa Maureen
Ada Shi 33	Campognone 144
Susan Chorpenning 36	Dixie O'Connor 147
Geoffrey Levitt 38	William Hemmerdinger .151
Emily Elisa Halpern 41	Linda Saccoccio 153
John Henson 45	Maria Laura Hendrix . .161
Susan R. Kaufman 49	Genie Davis 165
Sudrak Khongpuang . . .53	Barbara Kerwin 171
Barbara Nathanson 58	Debbi Green 177
Jodi Bonassi 60	Michael McCall 183
Linda Legman 63	Jesse Standlea 189
Leah Knecht 73	John Dingler 197
Marjan Vayghan 78	Robert A Costanza 199
Monica Marks 84	Mary-Gail King 206
Christianna Soumakis . .89	Kayla Cloonan 212
Simone Gad 96	Edwin Nutting 220
Cindy Zimmerman 100	Nancy Good 223
Stuart Rapeport 106	Debbi Swanson Patrick .230
Malado Francine Baldwin .110	Ginger Van Hook 235
Barbara Fritsche 114	Karrie Ross 239
Disha Dua 117	

Our Ever Changing World:
Through the Eyes of Artists

Artist Art & Story
A Moment in Time, 2020
International

Book #14

Laura Larson

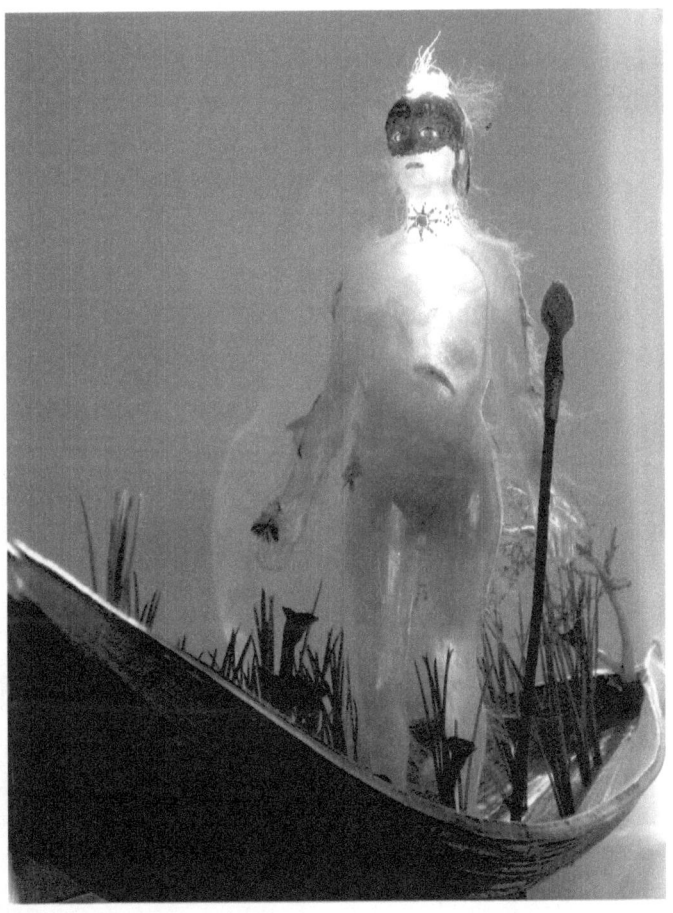

Name: Laura Larson
Discipline: Visual Artist
Country: United States of America

2020:
Several years ago, after my Mom's passing, I created a sculpture representing her last voyage in a "Viking" boat.

(We're Swedish.) During the quarantine my Mom – Elin – came to visit me.

Feeling a bit anxious like so many of us, I was looking for spiritual guidance to sooth my shattered nerves. I was drawn to a Numerology site on the internet and decided to hear a podcast on angels. While I was listening it suddenly stopped. Annoyed, I went back to see if I could pick it up again, but it started over at the beginning. This happened a couple of times. Finally I gave up and stopped, turned my chair around and noticed the wind blowing the curtain on the living room window, intermittently letting the light in at such an angle that it streamed through the sculpture on the shelf on the wall. I quickly grabbed my Iphone and managed to take several short, if shaky, videos from different positions in the room.

I wondered if it was one of my guides or perhaps the angel Gabriel that the Numerologist had been talking about. My husband, Dean and I remarked on how beautiful the light was and how rare an occurrence it was as the light had to be at a certain angle and the breeze had to blow at a certain velocity to get the curtain to move in and out. Strangely it took me a couple of days to realize that I had titled the sculpture "Light Bringer." In Welsh my mothers name, Elin means nymph, in Greek it means torch. Put together it felt like "Light Bringer" was a perfect name, because my mother brought light and love to everything she did and to everyone she knew. And then I understood that she was the spirit that had come to visit.

This experience made me feel as though the veil between here and "beyond" is very thin right now as we shelter at home, and that love never dies.

Website: http://www.larsonart.net

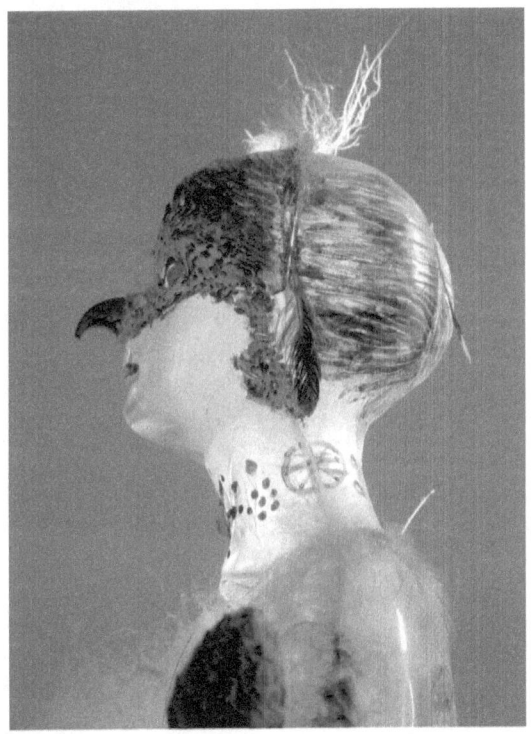

Our Ever Changing World: Through the Eyes of Artists: Book 14

Kerrie Smith

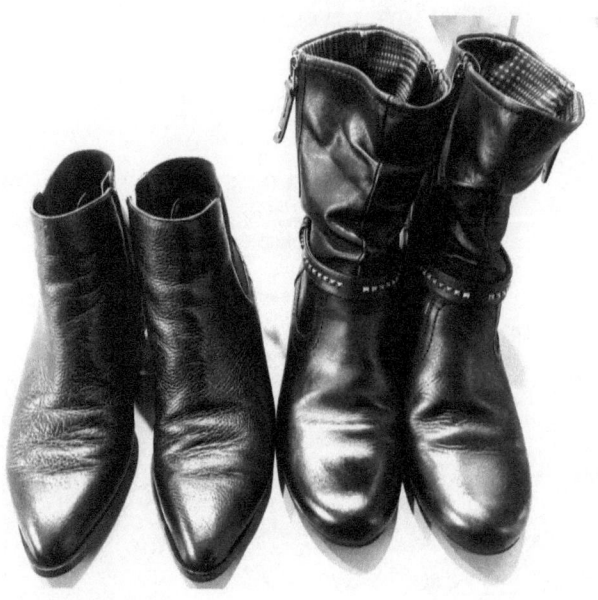

Name: Kerrie Smith
Discipline: Artist/Painter
Country: United States of America

2020:
Covid 19-Book Story-These Boots are Made for Walking

Strange times of repetitive motions, trying to keep busy, productive, but today I'm paralyzed and cannot get any further than my front door. No masked walk around my neighborhood today. Tomorrow possibly, a new day, and the next a new day and on and on and on. The name of days are no longer important or relevant. So what can I do? I've already cleaned out every drawer and cupboard, organized my closet, weeded my garden, cooked and cooked and cooked yet again. Drank another cup of English tea and dunked yet another Digestive Biscuit, oh boy my sweet tooth is taking over.

So new rituals are born, looking at old photo albums of my family through the decades, histories told of loved ones now gone and still greatly missed. Memories of my grandfather cleaning his leather boots in World War 2, spit and polish and again spit and polish, "so you could almost see your reflection in the toe of your own boot", he said. So there's my task at hand, I'm thankful that I can spit and shine my boots too, its bringing me comfort now. Sometimes those boots aren't meant for walking. They now stand as shining sentinels of boundless free wheeling treks into an unknown future.

Website: http://www.KerrieSmith.net

Our Ever Changing World: Through the Eyes of Artists: Book 14

Jan Book

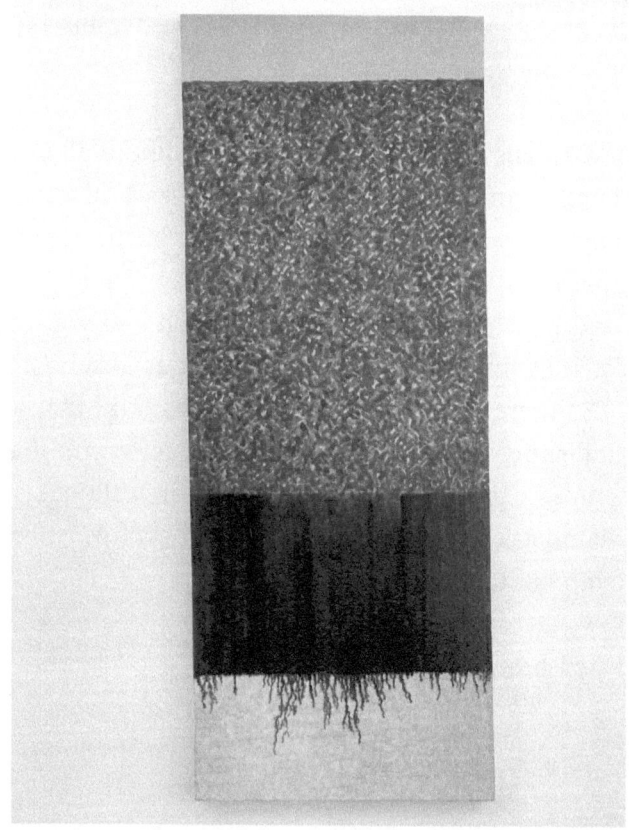

Name: Jan Book
Discipline: Painter/Writer
Country: United States of America

2020:
The Hedge in My Backyard and the Squirrels
By Jan Book
2/28/2021

Artist, ART, & Story: A Moment in Time, 2020: International

In 2018, I moved into a typical 1950's Southern California neighborhood of single-story ranch-style homes with long, deep overhanging eaves and sliding glass doors which opened onto a backyard patio. Most of the homes had a swimming pool, but our backyard just had the patio, a sweeping green lawn which ended at our neighbors back yard, and a 6 foot wood fence painted black. But behind the black fence was a solid row of 20 foot high ficus trees reaching up into the sky.

My first reaction was, "Wow, this hedge is tall", my second reaction was, "This could make an interesting painting", and my third reaction was, "But how do I capture the sense of size and the feeling of height?"

By March 2020, Los Angeles was in total lockdown and coping with the COVID-19 virus. Most of us were soon viewing our world from the inside looking out: no more shopping, no more dining with friends and family, or no more enjoying the many routines of our lives. And I still had not painted "The Hedge in My Backyard".

As time moved on, every day I would find myself standing by my patio windows and looking outside into My Backyard with the sun shining on the green grass, and just stare at the huge Hedge which was so tall, I could not see the blue sky above. Somehow, the mere presence of the Hedge gave me comfort. Perhaps it was the cool refreshing dark green color, or the strength of the large round trunks, or the massive wall of foliage protecting us from the forces outside which gave me a sense of stability and an assurance that the uncertainties of the health situation in our country would pass in time, and our lives would soon return to normal once again.

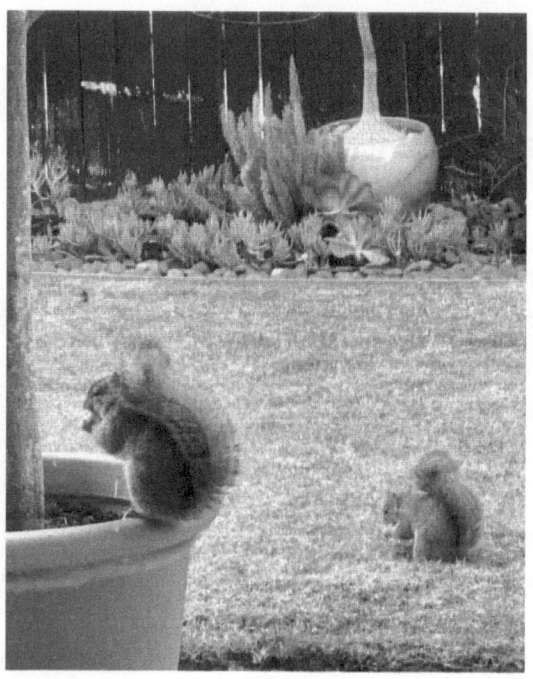

One day as I was looking out at My Backyard, I noticed a squirrel walking along the top edge of the black fence, scurry down a nearby small tree in my yard, and hop across the grass towards me. He had a very fat tail which he liked to wave back and forth as he stood patiently in the middle of the yard. Meanwhile, a second squirrel appeared but his tail was not as fat, and so I named the second squirrel, Skinny Tail and the first squirrel, Fat Tail.

I now had a reason to order "squirrel food" on line and proceeded to feed Fat Tail and Skinny Tail on a regular basis. And when I had fresh squirrel food for them, I would call them by name and soon they would appear to eat. (See photo, Two Squirrels Eating)

My intent was not to domesticate these squirrels, but I did like the idea of having them come into My Backyard and allow me to interact with them. Yes, this was a diversion from the isolation I was feeling because of COVID, and yes, it was thrilling to be able to feed and interact with a wild animal. And yes, when Fat Tail and Skinny Tail did not come to visit, I was disappointed and missed them.

From my perspective, these squirrels lived in The Hedge because that is where they came from and would return after each visit. For the squirrels, The Hedge was probably just protection which enabled them to move from place to place. But while the squirrels would come and go, it was The Hedge which became a source of entertainment and comfort for me, and my constant companion.

In June 2020, and as luck would have it, I was invited to participate in an "on-line gallery art show" titled, "Through the Window – An Artists View During COVID 19". And it was just that little push which I needed. I immediately accepted and began work on painting three versions of "The Hedge in My Backyard" (see photo, My Backyard #1, oil on canvas, 30"x12").

Website: https://www.janbook.com

Our Ever Changing World: Through the Eyes of Artists: Book 14

Sheila Fein

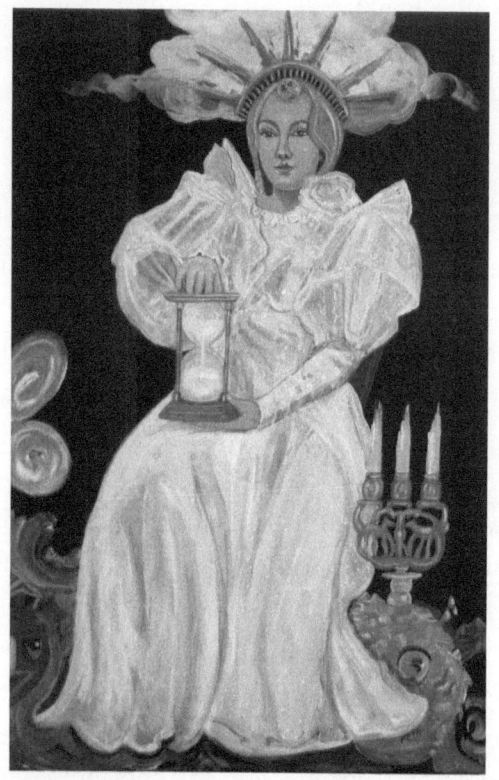

Name: Sheila Fein
Discipline: fine artist and illustrator
Country: United States of America

2020: A time to be present
By Sheila Fein

When we examine the timeline of our individual lives, we realize we share this timeline with every other living being on earth. In my view, when the world experiences tragedies, it feels like a deck of cards being shuffled and events happen, but not all at once. This has allowed the world in part to work on rebalancing. However, the present Covid-19 pandemic has brought the whole earth to its knees at the same time. The past year, 2020 showed me that it is going to take all of us to find balance again.

As an individual I find myself in a new normal where we are trying to isolate from one another, social distance, and wear a mask when outside and with others. All this to try and stop the spread of the disease. Though I am a lucky person who can isolate and do my creative work at home, I am overwhelmed with the impact of this virus personally and its impact on the world. Also, I have yet to recuperate from the period of time I was not able to be in my home.

From 2018-2019 I experienced the effects of the Woolsey Fire. This was a catastrophe affecting all of California, as well as the Santa Monica Mountains that I live in. I experienced a shock when we almost lost our family home, and my life's work as an artist since I was a child. The fire had left my home with burns and severe smoke damage, which made it impossible for my family and I to go home. The irony of this pandemic for me, is that after we could not live in our home for over 8 months, now because of the Covid-19 Pandemic, we could not leave it.

I went from an individual tragedy to our shared global one. These two experiences which came back-to-back for me, made time a surreal thing to me and had thrown off the rhythm and balance of my life.

Before the pandemic and after the fire, I had finally resurrected my Imaginings Sketch/People Sketchers figure drawing workshops which I held in my home studio for many years. I had persevered in rehabilitating my home and got back a semblance of my life.

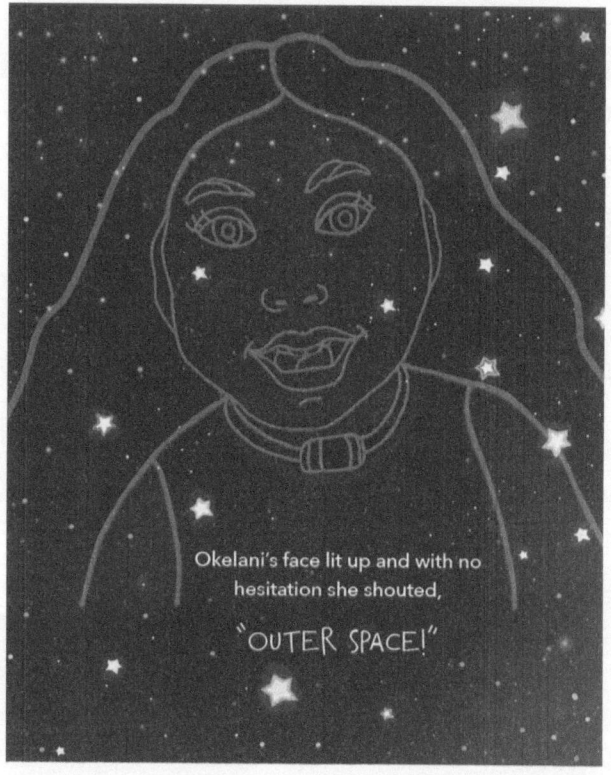

Okelani's face lit up and with no hesitation she shouted,

"OUTER SPACE!"

Since I am motivated by my love to create images, collaborate with other artists, and learn, this was a personal triumph. I was overjoyed to have my workshops back for myself and all who shared this with me. With the lockdowns and because it is unsafe to gather, I am unable

Artist, ART, & Story: A Moment in Time, 2020: International

to provide this venue at this time. I remain hopeful one day I can offer this again.

With my experiences that knocked me down from producing my work with a clear mind, 2020 became an anchor in time for that. Besides for my completed paintings and drawings, I had amassed many incomplete oil pastel, color pencil, and black line drawings from the time I had been running my workshops. Suddenly there was the time to work on them. The series are called; LA Models and the Red Couch, and Just a Line Series. This work has been my documentation of the living art models of our time in Los Angeles and the figurative art movement in our country. They are the model muses that are drawn in the Getty Museum, art schools, animation studios, and private workshops, as well as by individual artists. The work I am doing on these drawings and paintings are coming to fruition. I look forward to sharing them when we can all safely enjoy art shows again.

I have also been immersed in children's book illustration working with publishers and independent authors. I am proud of the two books that have been published this year. They are Okelani's Enchanted Wheelchair by Alexandra Sanchez and Three Booms! & A Plop by Nancy Goodstein. It was an honor to be part of Karrie Ross's Book #spareasquare, and to have my work sell at Gallery 30 South at their annual coaster show. Also, my drawing, Counting Ponies was included in The Joy of Art by Carolyn Schlam, one of the talented artists that came to my drawing workshops.

I have always been a tenacious person with my head down creating. This isolation has given me time with my daughter and my husband, as well as my lab, Charlie. but it has taken away my time with my other children, and friends. Most importantly it has taken away the hugs I love to have with my three grandchildren.

Now we are at the end of 2020 and living with all the virus has taken from everyone. Life has never felt more precious to me, time never felt so short.

I am hoping with the passing of 2020 and the coming of 2021, the new government of the Biden/Harris team will stop the chaos of the previous administration, solve the distribution problem of the vaccines that were just developed, and help to rebalance the world.

Though I continue to work alone in my studio, live on Facetime, the phone, and Zoom calls, I look forward to the world getting back on its feet and hope for a new plan that works for everyone. Time will pass and tell what will happen.

This pandemic has made me see our global connection as never before. There has been so much pain and death. Beyond myself and my individual experiences hope is returning in my heart. I am present and accounted for. I am working towards individual balance. The timeline of history never stops, but a giant asterisk will forever mark 2020.

It is my pleasure to submit to Karrie Ross's 2020 Book, my painting, Keeping Time-acrylic on canvas, 24 x 36" which is a painting about my obsession with time. I am also submitting one of my illustrations from the book Okelani's Enchanted Wheelchair to share a child's hope, joy, and the magic of outer space.

Please visit my website https://sheilafein.com/
and follow me on Instagram @sheilafein.
I would love to hear from you.

Best Wishes,
Sheila Fein

Our Ever Changing World: Through the Eyes of Artists: Book 14

Laurence de B Anderson

What to do at the border, what?
This is the battle of the battle,
and the border itself is full of time, or out of it:
waving hands, police around cars, turn-backs and shouted tears.
Indeed, when the neighbouring country was a king of death
and the roaring drinkers sang songs of happiness,
when last week my dog gave me meat from the neighbourhood,
and I didn't drink the house,
I felt we had a lot, you see, of water, toilet rolls...
But we didn't know who to believe, the cat or the singing tree,
or the rumours of ordinary people singing on their own.
We see the useless sky,
and ask, 'Please, sir, what time is truth?'
And, while remembered hurt is always new,
and the fairground experts gossip,
their rumours mounting to a fever of anguish,
the ravens croak down by the umbrous river
and Time...

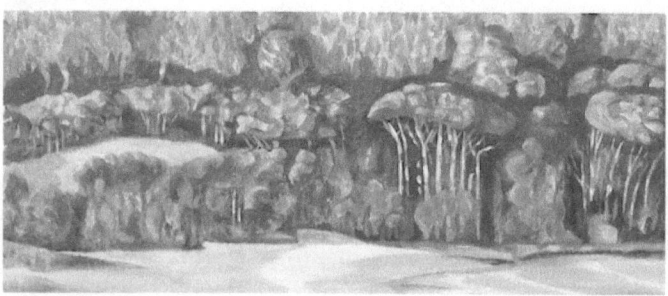

Name: Laurence de B Anderson
Discipline: poetry
Country: Australia

2020:
November saw the usual run of bushfires up and down Australia's east coast. No-one who was not directly involved paid them much attention at first. (It happens

every year, doesn't it?) But this year was different. We'd had years of drought, and the gum tree forest, vast and anonymous, had built up years of dry leaves and bark on the forest floor. Add to that the increasingly terrible summer heat with every passing year. So.. up it all went. Here, there and everywhere. The fire service made a website showing all the active spots — it seemed like the whole coast was on fire. Seen from space, a vast plume of whitish smoke blew towards New Zealand. On the ground people died, houses burned, animals burned, fire crews burned, whole suburbs and towns in the middle of nowhere burned. Every newshour repeated the same story, only it grew and grew like the fire itself, till it seemed there was no way anyone could escape it, and even the most insulated citizen in the middle of a wealthy suburb put a cloth across their face and began to look worryingly at the trees along the avenue, at the red sky, at the gentle snowstorm of ash flakes that fell in every suburb. Every person began to collect their most precious belongings: wedding albums, jewellery, passports, kids' photos, into a couple of suitcases. The incessant heat did not help, and the power began to fail as everyone turned on their air conditioners. I live in a leafy and wealthy suburb, but it's surrounded by native forest. I phoned my brother—no, I can't come to your daughter's wedding in New Zealand, the fires are getting closer. My wife went instead. I stayed indoors where it was easier to breathe, the garden being full of smoke under a red sky. I packed the precious belongings. I got out some cash, and filled the freezer. The shops were running low. Hundreds of flies were clustering round the front door, which was the coolest part of the garden. The cat was disturbed and maiowing incessantly. Every night, I got up at two a.m and got up on the roof with a hose pipe, soaking it in water, my eyes running from the incessant smoke. I blocked the gutters with old rags and filled them with water. After five days of the fire being within a few miles, and embers flying through the air with the strong wind, it all began to die down, and I was exhausted. My wife came back from New Zealand. Very few people were coming to see me at work (I am a family doctor). Then we heard on the news of a new virus out of China. It was the start of lock-down season. No-one knows when it will end.. In Australia lockdown has been haphazardly applied - some states are quite lax and others draconian in their approach. Everyone's arguing about it - but our statistics are quite good. This poem is my response to the virus... It is called 'Lockdown Protocol.' The painting is a little beach scene near Eden — this area is just black and brown now, having been totally burnt.

Website: http://www.maricom.com

Artist, ART, & Story: A Moment in Time, 2020: International

Ada Shi

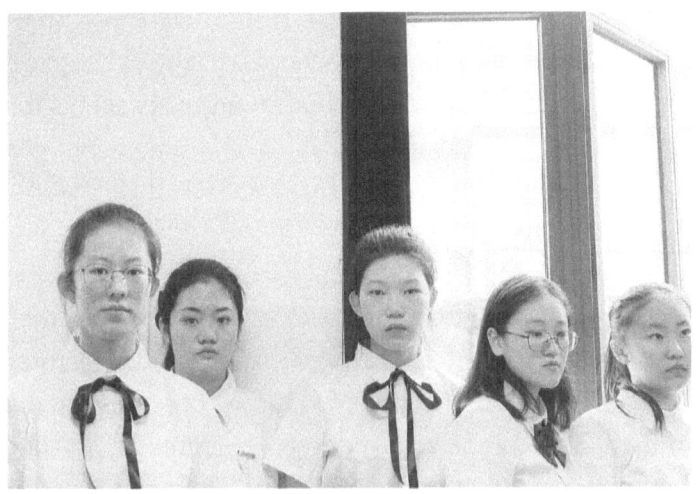

Name: Ada Shi
Discipline: photography
Country: China

2020:
In China, many people think that age 15 is the best time of life, because there is no need to worry about complex social relations, but only thing to do is just to STUDYING.

I remember when I was 15 years old, studying and participating in sports practice for the school team was a daily schedule; when I was criticized by the teacher for poor grades during class, I felt that the end of the world was coming; what I look forward to most every week is weekends and holidays. Because you can get rid of heavy homework.

These are most lives of the junior high school students in China 17 years ago.

I took pictures of junior high school students who graduated in the summer of 2020, but found many things that are different as the memories.

First of all, they are not happy.

The development of Chinese society is very fast. As there are too many needs from excellent talents in China at this era, a large number of well education becomes the first priority. The competition between students is not only about grades, but also directly related to the financial situation of each family and academic ability of their parents. In order to enter a better university or go abroad for further study in the future, Chinese children have been occupied most of their time by studying and learning other skills since they are in kindergarten. "Not to be left behind" has become a pressure for more than half of the families.

17 years ago, we still had weekends; we would love to make faces in front of the camera; and we were forbidden to use mobile phones in class. But now, they have no rest, study late in every day, and they also need to use electronic products to assist their learning in the class. Most importantly, expressionless were their most natural expression when they were looking at the camera .

Girls pick up their mobile phones to search for make up videos on Internet. They care that eyelashes are too short and ask me to Photoshop their photos.

This is a phenomenon in today's society: from parents to their children, are buried by the speed of country's development.

Most of them are living in the same lives, have the same thoughts and the same expressions.

We strive for the future, but we don't know what the future is.

Website:
https://mp.weixin.qq.com/s/PrKclvmXwZ4S0dElWHJ-yA

Our Ever Changing World: Through the Eyes of Artists: Book 14

Susan Chorpenning

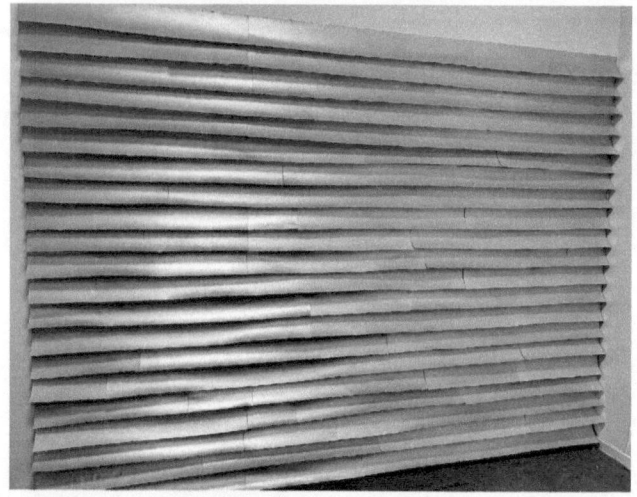

Name: Susan Chorpenning
Discipline: visual art
Country: United States of America

2020:
Writing a story about this year, I am certain I will remember two things.

Making art, and grief.

At first I made art obsessively, ordering extra supplies in case supply lines were cut off. Not only did I work a lot, but I made obsessive pieces with many parts, requiring many layers of paint. I always felt safe in the studio, no matter what was going on outside. Then, as reality set in, I slowed a bit, began to feel the sadness, the losses, the anger, the despair. I felt these for the many suffering so much more, while I was confined safely, more or less, in my studio. The pandemic was bad, the taking of Black lives was worse, and the the fires and smoke so close by added fuel to the grief, with politics and the loss of RBG forecasting a Stalinesque future.

Then, to make matters worse, I had to dismantle my studio of 18 years. It was for a long-planned and very good cause, demolishing and rebuilding the structure with room for me AND my partner, I alone having been blessed with the studio for so many years. But it's excruciating to sort old work, long-saved tools and bits of materiél, paper, paint, notes, that I might need someday. It became impossible to work in this space with piles of half-filled boxes. I'd begun making an interim space in the dining room, but it wasn't there yet. More grief. The studio and working, I hadn't realized how much they supported me.

But then, another thing had been supporting me to get into the studio, to generate patience, to contain the painful emotions and continue to go on each day. It was the source of the work in many ways, always about light. I'd been discounting it, but now, re-valuing it, the light. Not seeing it was what made those yellow-gray smoky skies so intolerable. I had to sit down, once again, and feel connection to the light internally, even as the externals changed and shifted. Meditation practice and the practice of art, connected. The sky begins to clear. We'll rebuild the studio. Artists can make work anywhere.

Website: http://www.susanchor.com

Our Ever Changing World: Through the Eyes of Artists: Book 14

Geoffrey Levitt

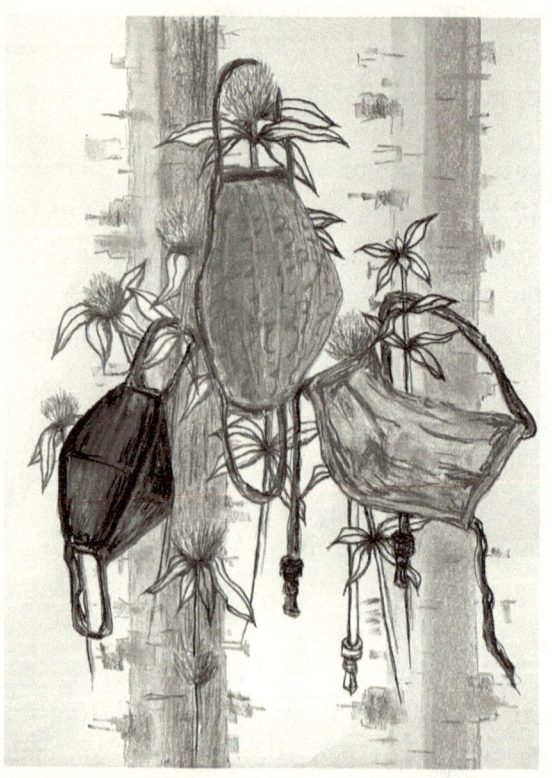

Name: Geoffrey Levitt
Discipline: Artist
Country: United States of America

2020:
Abundant Opportunities

There is abundant open desert and abandoned alfalfa surrounding our house. There are well traveled streets also. In this time of pandemic and economic slow down people dump and litter in these open spaces. Walking our chihuahuas sometimes twice a day, I find used COVID 19 face masks and gloves dumped here and there. I take photos of them and these inspire works of art back in my studio at home. There are times when finding face masks, being selective, I pick them up with a plastic bag. At home I wash them well, hanging them out to dry in the sunshine on our ornamental sage. They are often very colorful and not only are they wearable now, but also become subjects for paintings and drawings as well. By the way, the best natural sanitizer is sunshine. And our sage is a work of art itself with all the hanging masks. It also reminds me to put on a mask.

Going on we have bike lanes and other related traffic signs all over our neighborhood. Again out walking I find scenes of the bike lanes and the signage that also become subjects for art. Since bicycle sales are hitting records and as a means of transport are not polluting this seemed like a good subject for art as well. Furthermore all these activities can be accomplished in my home or close to home. No travel required. These activities have made a big difference in my attitudes about self isolating. My resourcefulness, something I've always strived for, has made for many a productive day spent this way. I used to collect recyclables in our park on our walks to not only make a little extra money but to keep our park looking nice. Alas, no more, since I am afraid of lurking COVID.

I have been self isolating throughout the Pandemic. Having my dogs has been a God Send to my sanity. Their walks force me outside and give me much needed exercise. As I am patent with them as they sniff their territory, they are patient with me as I photograph things of interest. The dogs miss being petted by everyone and contacts with other dogs, but still get to bark at all cats and dogs. I and my wife also sit outside on the patio with dogs in the evenings when we can. We have had to give this up because of the smoke from the fires.

We have a vegetable garden in pots, including peppers, tomatoes, mint, eggplant, and basil. Thyme and oregano. COVID has given me the time to actually garden. I share our excess produce with our neighbors and friends. Being in the desert many plants do not thrive. But we have found these grow well.

Mask using has become a way of life and almost a fashion statement. I have quit a collection to wear. I even do self portraits in them. I just need to remember to put them on and take them when I have to shop.

All in all COVID has certainly changed my life. Some in a bad way, but much in a good way. I have more time for my art. My dogs love me not leaving them alone. I am gardening. Will this never end?

Website: http://www.GeoffreyELevitt.net

Emily Elisa Halpern

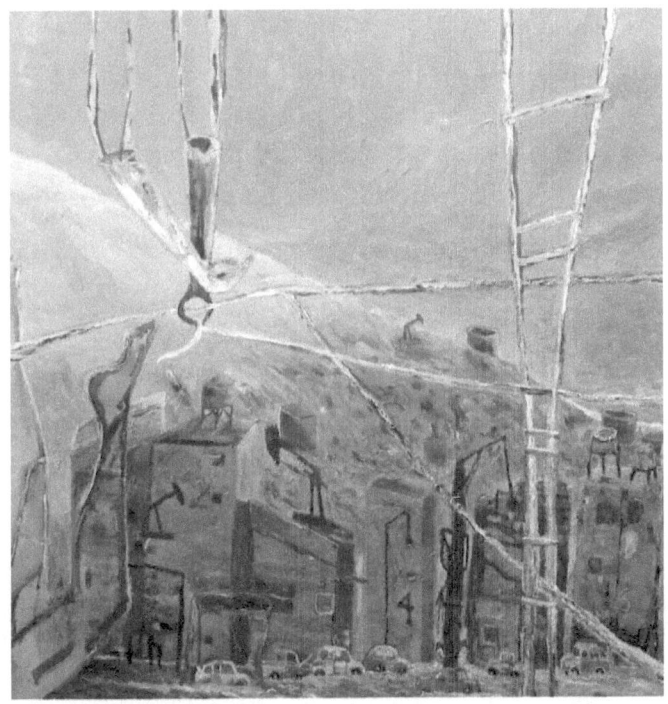

Name: Emily Elisa Halpern
Discipline: painting
Country: United States of America

2020:
I was in my art studio in Los Angeles when the pandemic panic first began in mid-March. My husband, who has had some serious health issues in the past, was at our house in San Diego. He was very concerned about the whole situation and, worried I might be ill somehow, wouldn't let me come home—as it wasn't clear how this

virus was spread or how to get tested. When I insisted on seeing him and drove back briefly, we looked through a closed window at each other and cried. Everyone and every surface seemed like a potential source of infection. I did some chaotic grocery shopping, tossing random items into my cart, trying to scavenge whatever was left on the shelves- and back at my studio, had a meltdown worrying about how to disinfect said items from Covid. Then the lockdown occurred. My sources of income came to an abrupt halt. I spent the next three months in my live/work studio and stayed put during that time.

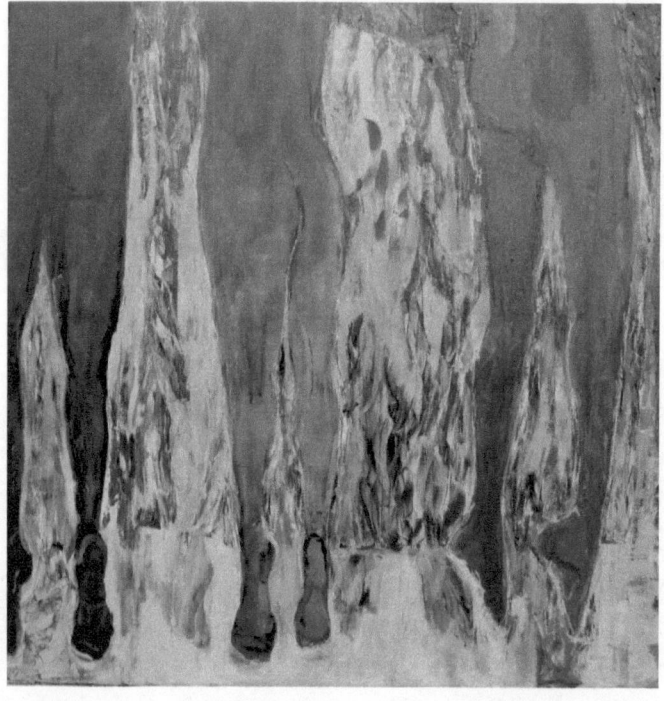

Though I didn't leave, the chaos and cacophony of the world around me- police helicopters overhead, sirens, raucous shouting - were clear and audible. I was glued to the news, watching our sad excuse for a President deny there was a problem as Covid deaths tolls rose exponentially. George Floyd's murder and then the resulting riots, fires and looting raised the stress. Two of my planned trips home to Canada were canceled when the borders were closed. I'm a terrible cook -or maybe I'm just emotional with a sensitive stomach- and ended up getting multiple cases of food poisoning. Without my usual hiking and gym routine, I became thin and somewhat gaunt. A family member in New York City died alone in a hospital. I stopped sleeping.

I painted, "End Times", 76" x 76", oil paint on linen, at the start of the pandemic. In the foreground, we see what I call "the fickle fingers of fate", (one mechanical in nature and the other making what could be interpreted as the white power sign), pull an acrobatic wire causing a figure on the left to trip and fall into the depths. In the lower background we see a reddish city scene. Smashed up cars and an oncoming flood of rolling water, indicate that all is not well. Upon closer inspection, the buildings are in disrepair and some are in the process of being smashed by a wrecking ball. Behind them, oil derricks clang on in their man-made destruction. I imagine a noxious smell.
Though there is a sense of doom, in the distance we see the yellow hills, of what might be Malibu. The skies are somewhat clear, but flickering rose. Perhaps more disaster will come from above. Perhaps disaster will come from below. The big one. An earthquake. Whatever happens, it will be okay. I have a sense of calmness and acceptance

now. I'm hiking in the mountains again and am more robust. Even if the situation is hopeless, I've had a marvelous life. The Earth will carry on without us and I sense that things will be better that way.

Website: http://www.emilyelisahalpern.com

John Henson

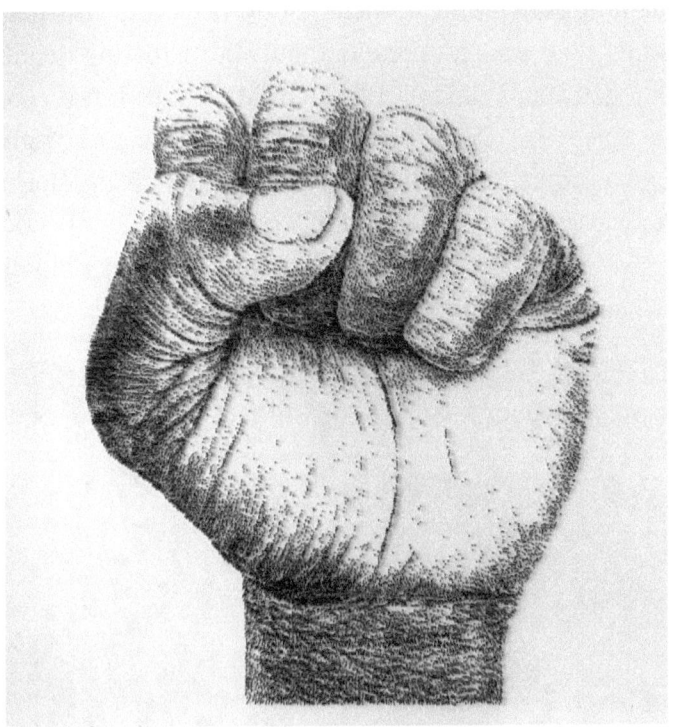

Name: John Henson
Discipline: Nail Art
Country: United States of America

2020:
This is nail art. And this one is made of 26,400 nails in a wood panel, and that number represents the amount of Black homeless people in Los Angeles last year.

2020 has been a profound year in so many ways. What really had a deep impact on me was the national outcry over systemic racism in our society, sparked by the killing of George Floyd by a police officer. I have participated in public protests before, but the coronavirus pandemic had me conflicted about participating in the demonstrations taking place in May and June. The Movement for Black Lives says there is no one "right" way to protest and urges everyone to "find your lane" to act against racial injustice. This sparked some reflection on my personal experience, and ways that I could contribute to this national discussion.

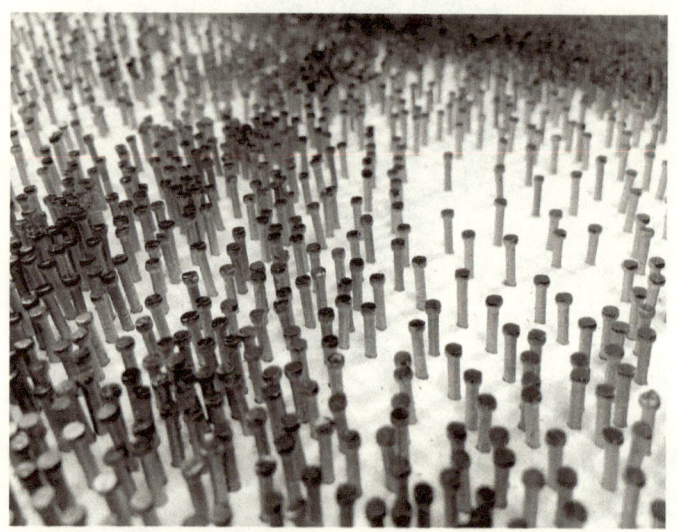

A quick back story…For nine years, my Saturday night ritual was to cook two pots of meatball stew, and early Sunday morning, to feed the homeless at a local park in West Los Angeles. I would meet up with my friend Martin, a former Catholic priest, who would bring a massive pot of steamed rice, paper plates and sporks to go along with my stew. On a typical Sunday, there would be around 50 people orderly lined up in front of our designated picnic table waiting for breakfast. Others would wait in the parking lot to carry supplies from our cars and set up the serving station. Martin would then offer a prayer, which was always extemporaneous and often topical. It amazed me how he could so consistently come up with words so eloquent and profound while I was not even fully awake. We would then serve up plates of hot food, and the hungry early risers would eat in small groups on the lawn or the surrounding picnic tables. It was a nurturing and nourishing ritual that I enjoyed being a part of. Afterward we would all clean up the area and disperse to get on with our day well before the park came to life with the usual Sunday family and sports activities.

Over the years I became familiar with many of the people who took part in this breakfast in the park, and grew to become friends with some. Something that became clear to me was that the homeless community included a disproportionate number of Blacks. Indeed, in Los Angeles a Black person is four times as likely to be homeless than a white person. And recently I learned that one of every three uses of force by the LAPD involves a homeless person.

The head of the Los Angeles Homeless Services Authority told the LA Times, "There is a staggering overrepresentation of Black people in homelessness, and that is not based on poverty, that is based on structural institutional racism."

So, what to do during these times? For me, creating a nail art piece was the easy decision – that's my wheelhouse. And I wanted to draw attention to our Black homeless community, since they are often considered the voiceless in our society.

I am fascinated with the idea of data driven art, so I decided to create a piece depicting the Black Lives Matter symbol and making it with a quantity of nails totaling the number of Black homeless in Los Angeles, according to a recent estimate.

Proceeds from the sale of this nail art piece will be shared with Black Lives Mater LA and the Shelter Partnership.

Website: http://www.johnhensonart.com

Susan R. Kaufman

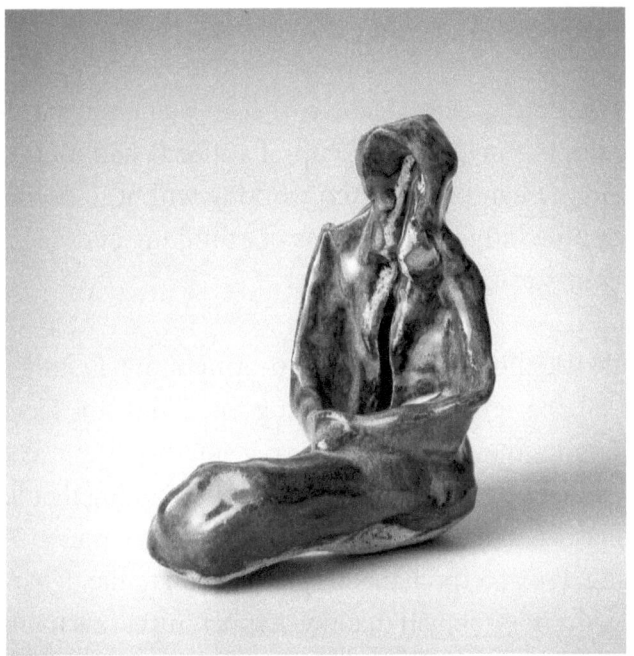

Name: Susan R. Kaufman
Discipline: sculpture
Country: United States of America

2020:
So much of my experiences during this Covid year has taken place in front of the TV watching the news. The news was so intense it was hard to leave, and little by little I realized how anxious it was making me. Hearing of all the deaths and running out of ventilators was making me more and more depressed.

This is a real life story of how my Covid sculpture came about and why the process was cathartic to me during this focus year.

This sculpture started out as I was watching the news and sipping my morning cup of coffee. I had a lump of clay in my hand and started working with it to become a sweet little kitty because I was not thinking of doing anything in particular.

While watching the news and hearing more about Covid and all the terrible things going on, I did not feel like making a cute cuddly kitten so I smashed my clay and saw something I was relating to. I kept working that lump of smashed clay with all the intensity of the emotion I was feeling. It was a spontaneous gut reaction to the ugly news of death, riots, and all that was happening at this time. To me, working in art is a way to help me understand, work things out, and to heal.

The word that kept coming up in my mind was "Dread." I don't believe I have ever even used that word before but I felt that word the entire time making this piece, so that became the title. It was an immediate translation between my mind and my fingers in working the clay to portray my emotions and feeling of dread.

This ceramic sculpture represents exactly what I was feeling during this Covid time. The deep crack you see in the center of the body with a trail of blood running through the middle core of the body and face, and a deep hollow where a face would be, is the feeling of ourselves changing course and being withdrawn from our neighbors with our masks and our distance.

Covid seems to be sucking out our life force and we don't know how to stop it. I feel there is enormous echoed grief with the human condition during this focus year. I heard from a relative working in the medical field putting patients on ventilators, she was so busy and working over time.

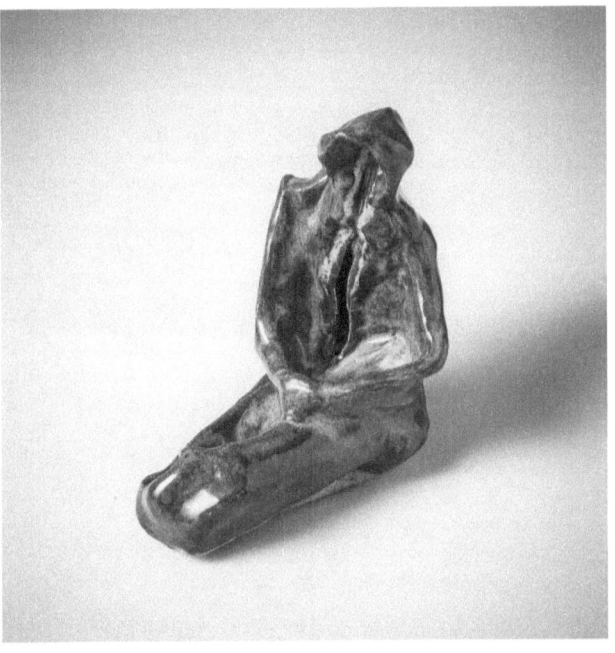

I hope my sculpture speaks of this time of Covid and political divide. I echoed this in my piece "Dread" with the large cut through the middle of the body. Through the act of spontaneously sculpting this piece, is when I realized what it was that bothered me and made me anxious.

Doing art is another way to think things out, understand more for myself, and maybe others might get a glimpse of what I see that they can relate to. Sculpting can be meditative to me, and in telling my story I hope you can see how unrealized anxiety festers inside and then when doing art work such as this one, at this time, it swam right out into this Covid sculpture "Dread."

Story and Art by Susan R. Kaufman
Photo by W. Scott Miles

Website: http://susanrkaufman.com

Sudrak Khongpuang

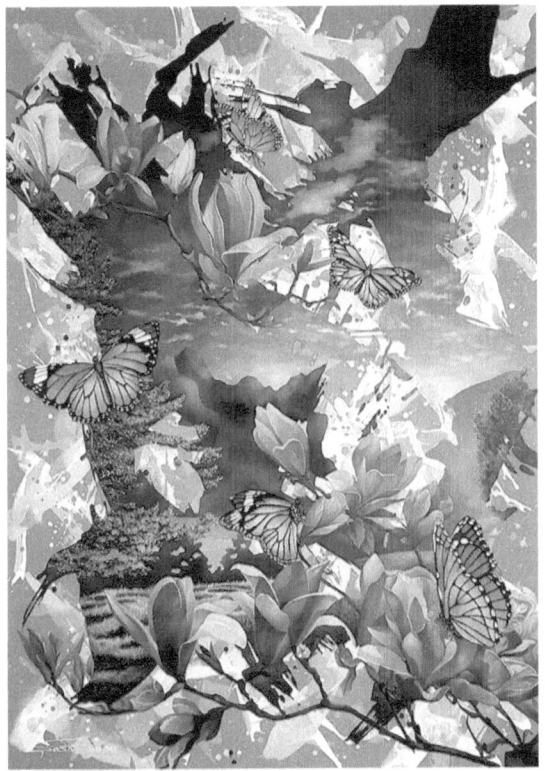

Name: Sudrak Khongpuang
Discipline: Painter, Visual artist
Country: Thailand

2020:
"The visitor"

On a day when everything was silent, people stayed in their own homes. They avoided meeting during the spread of the coronavirus situation.

I was able to get the sound of birds chirping, the wind, and even the sound of falling leaves scraping down the concrete road in front of the house. It was a good time that I would sit down and use my thoughts to consider the reasons why we were born and lived on this planet.

We all know that "Earth" was born around 4,600 million years ago, and that the first human species arose about 200,000 years ago when compared to what we spent only 0.004% of our time on this planet. Therefore, we cannot claim that is the king of the earth. we can say that we are only temporary visitors.

How about us as visitors, good or bad for the earth?

When viewed from the reduced amount of natural resources, the number of names of endangered species is increasing. Changing climate There is an increasing amount of pollution in both water, air and soil. Ecology is being damaged. So we cannot call ourselves a good visitor to the earth. On the other hand, humans have done different things. That is cruel to this earth.

And what about the earth ... Has the world sent a warning to us to be aware of our own actions? If we look back at the past we can see that humanity has faced many natural disasters and epidemics. Which may be a warning that the earth has sent to us that What we do to the earth finally, it comes back to us.

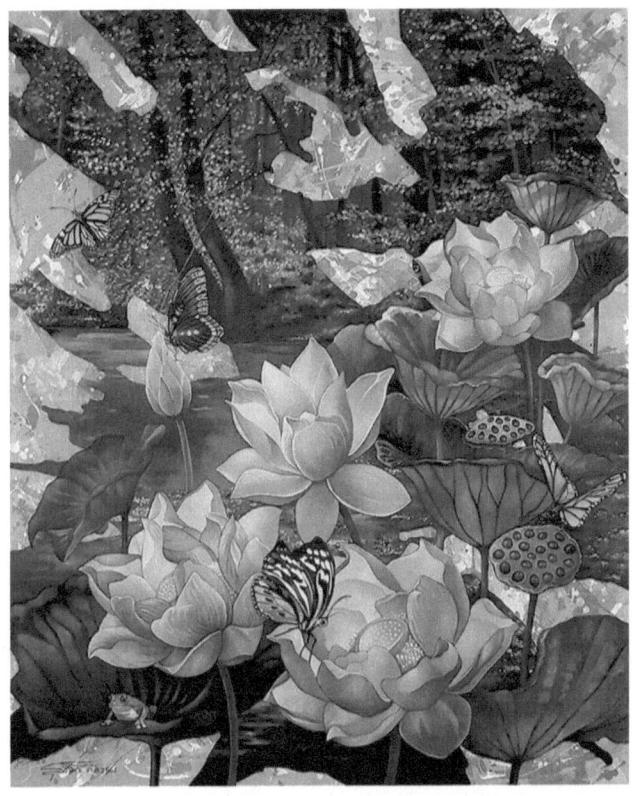

In my living time, the planet has taught me to know a deadly crisis from coronavirus. Its lethal force has made many humans around the world to adjust their behaviors. We must reduce traveling, reduce socializing and we choose to shop more online. In order to reduce going out of the house. We are paranoid of each other, and worried that someone would bring the coronavirus to our body? For almost a year, the Coronavirus has visited all of us. All races, genders, and ages are exposed to the effects of the coronavirus. Some of us were ill, Someone even died, and almost all of the people were affected by the economy as the city shut down, in order to reduce the spread of this virus.

While humanity is struggling in any way to defeat this virus, we have seen another side... the natural environment and the animals including water and weather conditions have returned much better than before. The ocean returned to a bright blue color. Dolphins swim happily, the sky is clean, fresh air because the smoke from cars has reduced. It reflects how much human beings have persecuted the planet even though we are just visitors.

Although in the future we had a vaccine to fight the coronavirus. And we will be able to come back to life normally again. But from this crisis, we need to be more aware of the conservation of the environment and natural resources. Because we are only visitors. And do not know what the world will send something to warn us in the future.

Because.... at some point in the future, the human race may be extinct. But this planet will be perpetual.

I heard the sound of leaves scuffing against the street in front of the house. A butterfly flew to a small tree by the window. I turned back and looked at the canvas and reached for the palette and brushes. I paint the colors green, blue, pink, and yellow in the form of a blooming flower.... raise a bouquet to the sky show off its beauty to face the clouds that rise above.

I am one of the visitors to this earth, who are also creating works of art. I hope the art I create will outlast my life for the next hundreds of years. My art offers a positive view of nature and to offer the beauty that is possible. So that we all realize the importance of nature. If nature has lost its balance then humans will also suffer. And that might be the end of the human race.

Website: http://www.sudrakart.com

Our Ever Changing World: Through the Eyes of Artists: Book 14

Barbara Nathanson

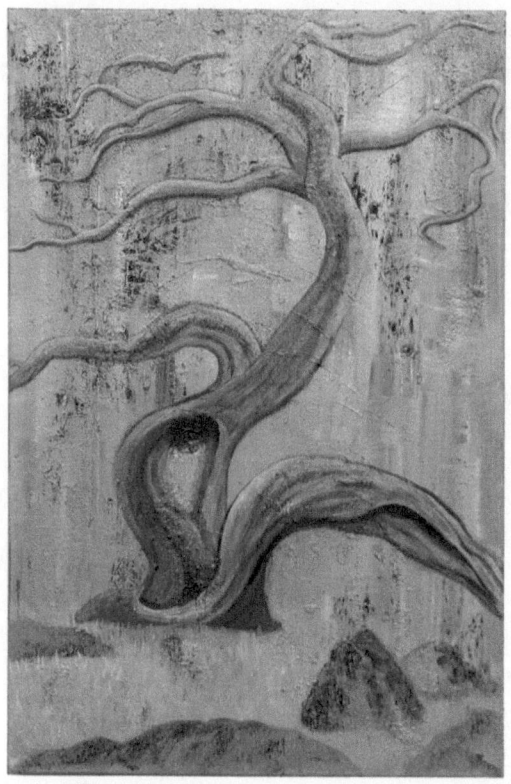

Name: Barbara Nathanson
Discipline: Painting
Country: United States of America

May 2 at 3:17 PM
During this time of quarantine I have spent a lot of time in my studio (which is at my home) painting, staring out the clerestory, watching the clouds go by while a layer of paint dries, then adding another layer of paint. Some days

I read, listen to audio books while I clean house then I head back to the studio to paint some more. I have enjoyed having no schedule to adhere to and not clock watching but just doing what moves me when it moves me. I stay up late, sleep in, have meals at random times. It seems like a vacation from responsibilities and social expectations. I never know what day it is but reality hits when I must go out to get groceries, I am worried about picking up this dratted virus and bringing it home. I turn on CNN &/or MSNBC and am filled with dread. My dreams are full of fears and tension. I feel this need to paint each day to bring calm and hope back. Once started my paintings flow easily as they are of aspects of nature that have an element of peace and calm in their beauty. I lose myself in the image growing on my canvas. I need this to counteract the disturbing feelings of life careening out of control outside my studio, outside my house, in the world. My name is Barbara Nathanson

Website: www.barbara-nathanson.com/

Jodi Bonassi

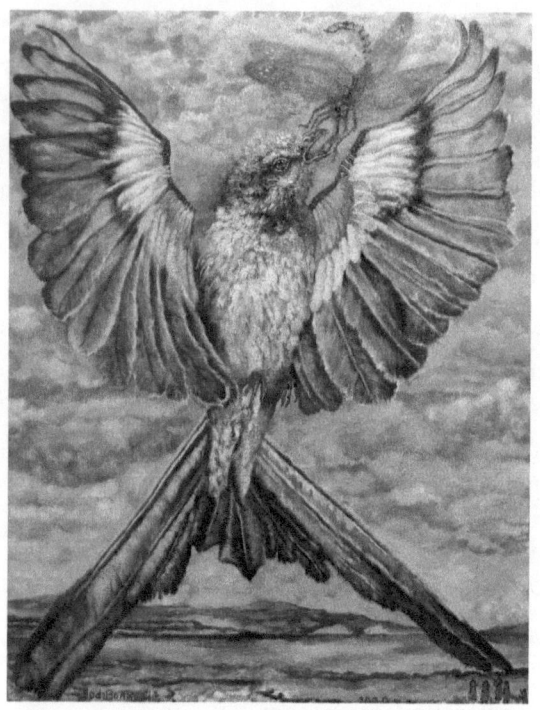

Name: Jodi Bonassi
Discipline: Visual Artist- Painting and Drawing
Country: United States of America

2020:
After the shutdown I went to the market to get milk and a few other items. These were the first days of April 2020. It felt like the end of the world. People were running up and down the aisles hoarding, loading their carts with extras of everything. It was early in the day but many items were already gone. I froze in an aisle, staring at

empty shelves, and watching people grab for things. I felt my own mounting panic. A few people were arguing over toilet paper. There was a tall beautiful black woman standing in the check out line. She wore sweats and seemed exhausted. I wanted to talk to her and draw her. She had long cornrows and large luminous eyes. My thought was, "She is someone's daughter and maybe a mother." An older man stood next to her via social distancing. He walked with a cane and seemed so fragile. I wondered if he was homeless or well cared for. Even with the masks I could see these people on a deeper level. I could see the woman's eyes brimming with tears waiting to fall. I felt the sting of my own tears. We nodded to each other. I wish I could have hugged her. Afterwards I sat in my car in the parking lot. By that time the tears were streaming. It took a few minutes before I could drive. In the first months of the pandemic I made a few large paintings. One piece was about the woman at the market. Another painting depicted the BLM protests by the White House Fence. It seems so wrong to call it a "White House". The death of George Floyd on camera brought to light the lack of freedom in the world. Continued racism is hidden under the guise of equality that does not exist. But in this new reality there is a hope for people to be truly free. People came together from all walks of life. The darkest periods in history can bring the light of positive change.

Now I draw birds. I think about how animals live each moment and go with what ever that moment dictates. I want to inspire others to love and cherish beauty in the world. True freedom is when we allow each other the same freedom to fly and be who we are. I can't wait for the day when I can visit my son and give him a huge hug without a mask. This time has reminded me that real love is unconditional. Love is the most precious gift we can give is each other.

Website: www.jodibonassiart.com

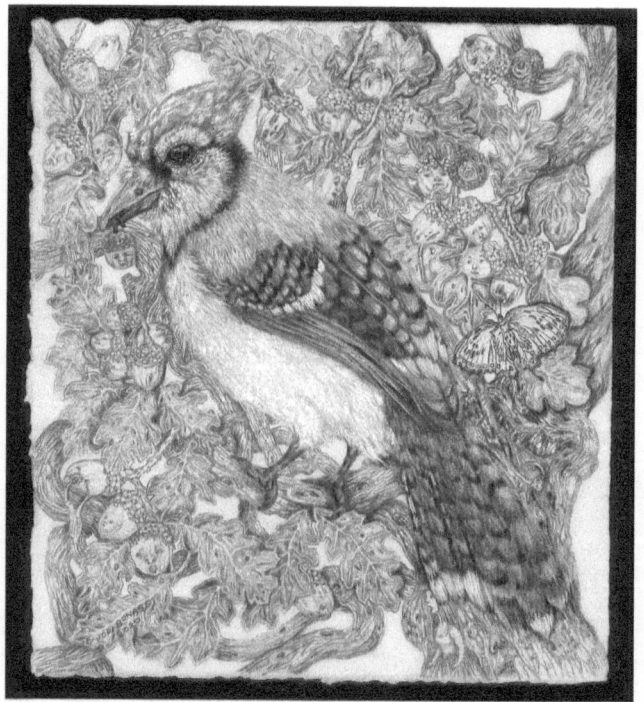

Linda Legman

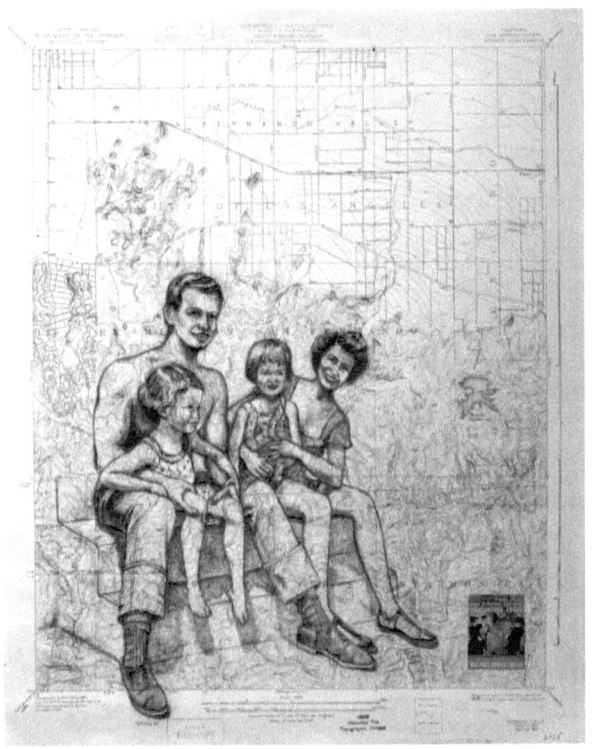

Name: Linda Legman
Discipline: 2 D Art
Country: United States of America

2020:
One of my favorite quotes is, "When one door closes, another opens, but sometimes the hallway's a bitch." 2020 has been a bitch of a year.

The most profoundly upsetting events of 2020 for me were:

1) The murder of George Floyd and Breonna Taylor which alerted the world to the systemic and overwhelming racism in the USA.

2) A world-wide pandemic of Covid 19 that has killed over 2 million people to date and now has 98 million confirmed cases sick, causing many to suffer lifelong complications. The end is not in sight.

3) The worst president the United States has ever seen. I will not say much about him in this writing, but he exacerbated many people's stress.

My life is affected every day by what is happening around me. Sometimes the results are incapacitating: I came down with a case of shingles two days after the slow knee-to-neck murder of an unarmed Black man, George Floyd, by a White policeman, was captured on video for the world to see.

A week after I started on antivirals for my shingles, I broke out with painful hives. The hives continued on and off for the next six weeks. During that time Breonna Taylor, a Black woman EMT, was shot to death in her bed by White Police. The news continued with more murders by police of unarmed Black folks. The news made me sick. Literally.

Artist, ART, & Story: A Moment in Time, 2020: International

Black Lives Matter and other civil justice groups took to the streets to protest the continuous murders of unarmed Black folk in our country by racist police who are not held accountable for killing people of color. Getting away with murdering Black folks is just one part of the systemic racism that is America's history.

Because of the pandemic, I did not physically join any peaceful protests, as much as I wanted to show my support. What could I do to help? More and more of America's systemic racism was exposed but one really hit home:

I learned that eight million White WWII veterans got G.I. Loans, but out of 1.2 million Black soldiers less than 100 got them. Less than 100. Outrageous injustice. My father was one of the eight million veterans who benefited, so I knew that I could tell this story through art.

I grew up in a darling house in Reseda, CA. My parents qualified for a G.I. Loan in 1950 because my father was White and had been a 101st Airborne Paratrooper who jumped in Normandy on June 6, 1944. With home ownership, my parents became middle class with all the benefits that entailed: A good education, living in safe neighborhoods, employment opportunities, good health care, and financial security, to name a few.

Guaranteed G.I. Loans in Reseda, 1950 (if you're White) is drawn in charcoal with a tiny photo on vellum of a poster put out by the Veteran's Administration. I drew a picture of my family from a photo taken in 1952 of the four of us happily sitting on the back steps of our home in Reseda. The poster reads, "Veterans-if buying a Farm, Home or business learn about Guaranteed Loans. Contact your nearest office of the Veteran's Administration."

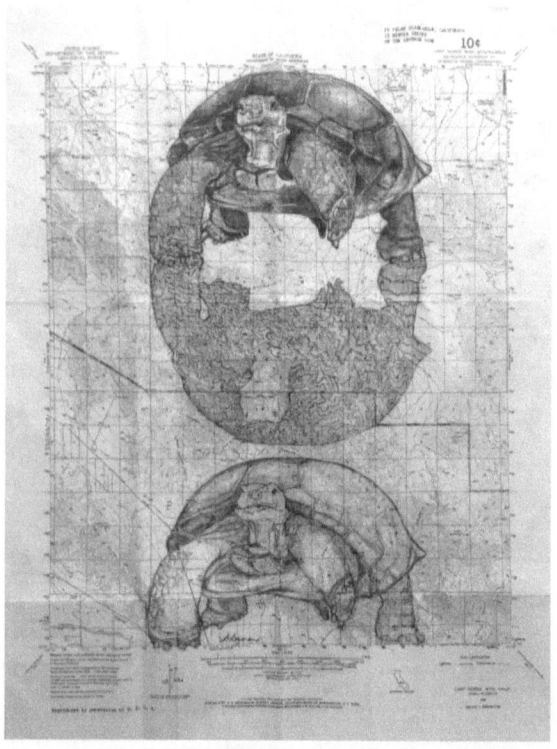

In this bitch of a year, 2020, I started making pictures that are intended to stimulate the viewer into asking deep questions about our history as Americans and our responsibility as human beings. I hope Guaranteed G.I. Loans in Reseda, 1950 (if you're White) stimulates questions that help lead to solutions for righting this wrong, making retribution, and contributes to ending racism once and for all.

It is important to address how profoundly my life has been affected by the Covid 19 pandemic that is crippling the world. The United States has lagged behind the rest of the world because our president and his blind followers have ridiculed worldwide health mandates to wear masks, wash hands often, and maintain "Social Distancing." Social distancing meant the end to social gathering.

Until this pandemic, I played pickleball with friends every week and had a busy professional and social life. Every activity was enjoyed without the concern of contracting a disease that could be fatal or cause permanent damage.

Before the pandemic I had a weekly Tuesday night art Painting Workshop taught by Barbara Shannon. I had been attending her workshop for about twenty years. When I was teaching full time, this Tuesday night workshop was often the only opportunity I had to make art. Barbara Shannon is a terrific artist and a wonderful teacher. Even after I got my studio at Studio Channel Islands, I continued attending her workshop for her insights, knowledge, and expertise, as well as the camaraderie of the other artists. I started my Vintage Map Series in this workshop.

The 2020 pandemic also stopped the weekly gathering at the studio of Sheila Fein where we drew artist models every Wednesday morning for three hours. I usually went to the beach afterwards to walk joyfully in the foam and look for dolphins. I still try go to the beach about once a month. The beach recharges me.

Before the pandemic I taught a painting workshop once a week at the Senior Center in Thousand Oaks through Conejo Valley Adult Education. I really enjoyed teaching adults after so many years teaching children.

The pandemic has forced me to do all of my business and community work over the computer with Zoom and Facebook (via computer).

Socializing is on the telephone or FaceTime (via cell phone). Rarely do we meet in person; always with masks, staying at least six feet apart, outside or in a large room with doors open.

I am one of the Artists in Residence at Studio Channel Islands Art Center (SCIART) in Camarillo, CA, who now gather for meetings through Zoom. SCIART's Black Board Gallery exhibits and other artist events can be accessed through our website videos studiochannelislands.org . Our Holiday Market 2020 was online because our center is closed to the public until we "flatten the curve" of Covid 19. Closing museums and galleries are mandates from the Ventura County Health Department and our conscientious Governor Gavin Newsom.

There are about forty artists with studios here, and over a hundred other artists who are members of SCIART. Before Covid 19 we had monthly Open Studios where the public could come to see, and hopefully buy, our art. Now we are closed to the public.

Like many artists, I post my new art on Facebook and Instagram under Linda Legman. Since we don't have Open Studios, it's a way for me to show what I am working on and get feedback from my followers. People can also see and buy my artwork from my website, lindalegman.com. I will be expanding it to include more information about each piece and I am considering starting a blog.

I made only one sale this year because of a contact through Facebook from an old friend who inquired if I still had a drawing that she had wanted since 1979. Even though I have not sold any other art in 2020, I was in several shows and was published in a book.

I was delighted to be in three different juried exhibitions in 2020 where I entered images from my Vintage Map Series: The Hillcrest Center for the Arts in Thousand Oaks invited me to hang eight images for "I Have a Story" in January; A remarque of Buttonwillow Tule Elk was shown at The Collectors Choice at SCIART in March; Triple Topographical Tortoises was juried into The Next Big Thing 2020 at the Blackboard Gallery at SCIART in August. However, no receptions were held for any of them because of Covid 19.

All receptions in galleries ended up being cancelled this year because of the pandemic, but the shows were still hung. All three shows posted the images virtually. Cancelling receptions was unfortunate, not only because receptions are fun, but because they draw crowds of art lovers who may be exposed to your work for the first time, and they are an opportunity for people to buy your work. Seeing small images on a computer is not the same as seeing the work in person. It's just not.

I had fun drawing my self-portrait on a single piece of toilet paper that was published in a book by Karrie Ross entitled, #spareasquare When toilet paper was seen as a rare commodity in May.

Expressing gratitude for all the good in my life is important. I am especially grateful to my wonderful husband, Robert Thompson. He loves and encourages my art. He is a fabulous chef, my tech support, and a wonderful life partner.

I am grateful for enduring and beautiful friendships. Especially during this 2020 pandemic year, my dear friends have helped sustain me, even though we could not be physically together.

I am grateful that I have a studio away from home that I can go to whenever I want because I don't share it with anyone. I moved into my studio at Studio Channel Islands Art Center (SCIART) in Camarillo, CA last year. I can go from my home to my studio without running into another person. I do share a foyer with a terrific artist who has the studio next to mine. We wear masks and stay at least six feet away when we talk. So, I interact in person with my husband at home and Gale Fulton Ross when we are in our studios.

I go to my studio at least five times a week to work on my Vintage Map Series, with forays into other artwork when so moved. I spend hours drawing or doing research in order to make the drawings more meaningful. Sometimes I just sit in my studio, surrounded by artwork, feeling blessed.

I have been working on my Vintage Map Series for three years. At the end of 2017 I inherited a series of California camping maps that were used by my father-in-law back in the 1950's. I draw animals in charcoal directly on these old maps. Each animal is drawn on a map that contains their habitat. Until this year, the series has focused mostly on California endemic, threatened and endangered animals. The California grizzly bear is the only extinct animal in the series. We must stop the further extinction of our beautiful California wildlife while we still have time. I am passionate about promoting the protection of wildlife through my art.

The series first started with my drawing on 20 x 26 inch California camping maps that were in a folded set. Besides the set of camping maps, I also inherited different kinds of maps to use. In the varied collection of maps I found a 17 x 22 inch topographic map produced in 1958 of the Mojave Desert area of Twenty-Nine Palm by the United States Geological Survey (U.S.G.S.). I had wanted to draw the threatened Mojave desert tortoise for two years and this map was perfect.

Triple Topographical Tortoises is the first of this series of California animals to be drawn on a topographic map. This drawing inspired me to order a map of Reseda from the U.S.G.S. in order to draw Guaranteed G.I. Loans in Reseda, 1950 (if you're White).

I am pleased to submit both of these charcoal drawings on topographic maps for this 2020 book for Karrie Ross.

I want to end this writing with another of my favorite quotes, "It always works out in the end, and if it hasn't worked out, it isn't the end yet."

I am hopeful that with the new administration of Joe Biden and Kamala Harris (America's first Black/Asian woman Vice President!) it will work out and the world will be a better place for all of us.

@lindalegman
Website: http://www.lindalegman.com

Leah Knecht

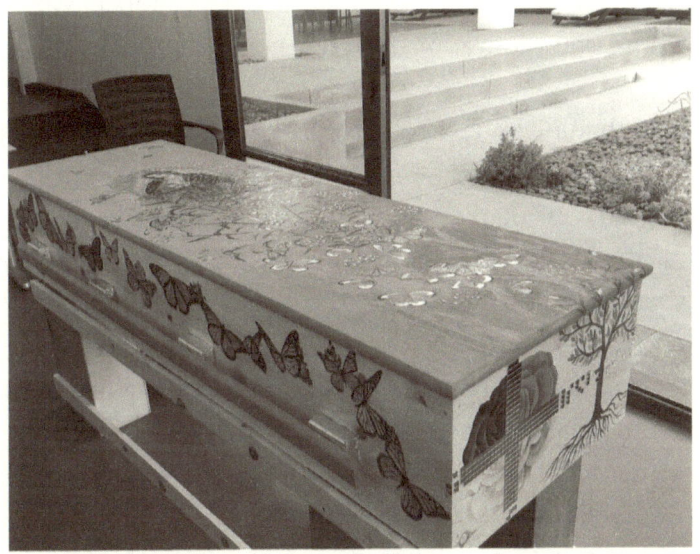

Name: Leah Knecht
Discipline: Visual Artist
Country: United States of America

2020:
As the year comes to a close, it is finally hitting me emotionally, after seeing the inequities in our communities in a span of 2 days. I saw my neighbors from across the street, swing dancing on Christmas Eve. They looked so happy and safely cocooned in their million-dollar home. Contrast that with my driving down Allen Avenue in Pasadena the day after Christmas and seeing an emergency call for what looked like a homeless man, body prone on the sidewalk, head on the street. Fire truck, paramedics, and police, and the guy looked stiff,

maybe dead. Right in front of the Eddie Van Halen memorial site at the liquor store, where mourners gathered by the dozens for Eddie when he died in October. Would anyone ever mourn for this poor homeless soul?

Later that night I watched the mediocre new Wonder Woman movie, and started crying. Not because it was that bad, but the boredom allowed my mind to wander, first to the scenes from above, and then the memory of experiencing the death of a dear friend last February.

Her name was Chantal, and she was a very gifted artist whom I met through a local Open Studios Tour. She, another artist and I decided to start what we named the "Women's Art Circle," because we found ourselves feeling isolated due to of the nature of our work. We invited 4 other artists who lived nearby, and the goal was to support each other through studio visits, critiques, and other art-related activities, but soon enough, we became close friends. Our lunches were filled with gut-busting laughter, and lots of cussing, with Chantal in her upscale clothes, impeccable hair and make-up, joining in. It was always a delight to hear her cuss in her lovely French accent! She cherished these times, and when she knew her battle with cancer was near the end, she summoned us to one last lunch at her home.

After lunch, she asked us for a favor, and that was to paint her coffin because she wanted it to be beautiful—not somber. We then looked at coffins online to see what would work for this purpose.

Then a few of us stayed, and helped her finish gluing medical disposable items from her treatments to a piece she had started, and was too weak to complete by herself. The items were the border, and her under-painting was the center, which is still unfinished. She seemed relieved though.

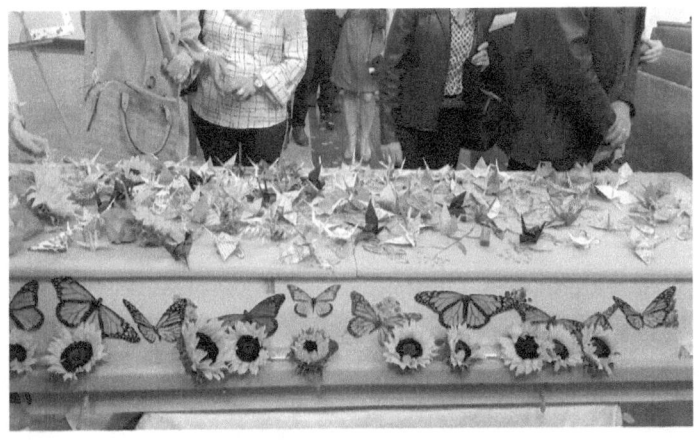

We worked on her coffin for about a week, as she watched from her bedroom across the courtyard. She "art directed" through the photos we showed of our daily progress, and she had some specific requests, but other details she left up to us. She loved Monarch butterflies because of the metamorphosis they undergo, so that was a unifying theme. She asked for the Virgin of Guadalupe, even though she had renounced her Catholic upbringing. Each of the 4 women who were involved basically took a side to decorate. We included a reproduction of her painting called the "Sleeping Beauty" a Tree of Life, and many Monarchs, plus my representation of our "Circle," a multi-colored rose, dissected by a plus sign–stronger together.

Her family had flown-in from France and England, and were there daily, watching our progress. They had their leisurely lunches on the patio outside the studio, and the table was always properly set. They even brought us tea trays, though they were so distraught, manners were innate. They have a very different lifestyle than we do, and it's inspiring.

We saw her get weaker every day, and she passed 45 minutes after we finished. I like to think she waited until it was done before she could let her own metamorphosis happen, and she could leave her pain-ridden body.

It was a profound experience, and I was honored to do it for her, but it was also incredibly painful. Still miss her, and think of her often. 3 other friends passed away this year, but to be with someone in their final days and hours was new for me. She was so brave, and worried about others more than herself in those last days, and even gave me a gift that helped me financially when I needed it most, though she could barely speak at that point. I will never forget her generosity and love.

This was right before lockdowns started, and since then I've kept my chin up, just in survival mode. I've been keeping busy, and entertained by my wacky chickens and wonderful dogs. While outraged by what Trump and the GOP have been doing, I haven't been as sad as I was last night. It hit home to think of all the lives that have been lost or destroyed this year, and how many people are mourning family and friends like I am mourning my beautiful friend Chantal.

Each life is precious. Let's try to be kind to one another in these difficult times, because you don't know what someone else is going through. We will get through this eventually. Looking forward to better times, my friends!

Website:
https://www.leahknecht-art.com/

Our Ever Changing World: Through the Eyes of Artists: Book 14

Marjan Vayghan

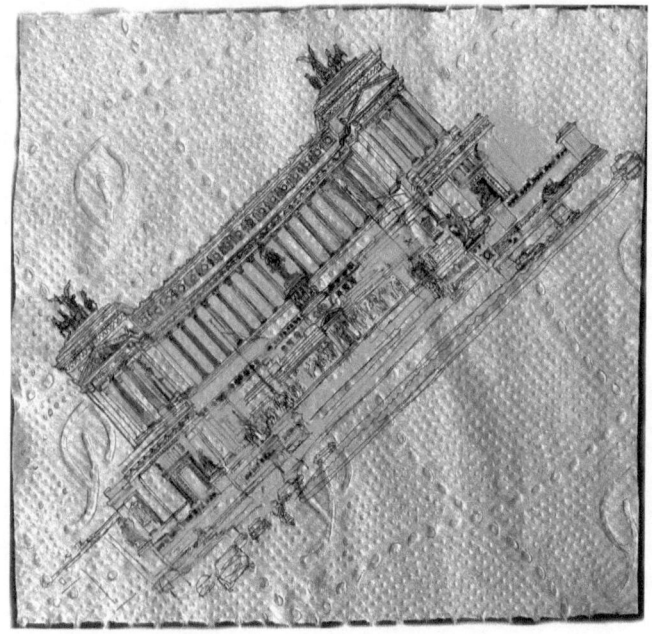

Name: Marjan Vayghan
Discipline: Conceptual artist/designer
Country: United States of America

2020:

Our family's Covid-19 2020 experiences were foreshadowed on Jan 27th, 2017, as "Chump" (the 45th president of the United States) signed his first Ban into law. That's the night my uncle was taken away with one signature. He had every right under the law to be in America with his wife and their son who is a medical professional, currently risking his life in our hospitals, where he is a citizen. "Chump's" actions of separating families and friends began in January of

2017. Three years later, now we have children in $775.00 a night cages. Some children have died and are continuously dying alone and sexually assaulted after being ripped from their families (and protectors) arms. We all stood by and did nothing. Now our elders, many of whom voted for "Chump", are dying alone in ICUs. Nation wide, faces are turning blue and expiring due to lack of ventilators, oxygen, Tylenol, our hospitals are out of the most basic resources. While the Federal gov outbids the States, and Kushner in charge of distribution of the goods is on record saying "These are our stuff, not the state's stuff." Our doctors and nurses risking their own lives are dying due to lack of basic protective equipment. Our nations answer to these brave souls is calling them "front line solders," in order to diminish their lives value and normalize their deaths. Akin to the bloodshed and mass loss of solders lives in a war zone. Well guess what that's wrong, their loss of lives doesn't have to be unavoidable! Basic protective equipment can help them! Just like you need real leadership, ventilators could be provided to the sick to help them get through this pandemic by lending them breath!

I'm writing you from my art studio, where this square of toilet paper art is coming into life surrounded by artworks and remanence of life, left behind by my best friends from school and life. Who had to leave the country suddenly under our current mango Mussolini in the White House. Children who were raised in America from an early age, how have only known America as their homes, who had to move to South Korea , Iran, Europe, Canada, and South America from fear of ICE separating their families. Great people who have worked and lived in America legally for years, then started getting harassed around 2017, till fear pushed them outa our country to places on the world that they have never lived or speak the languages of. I sit in this art studio worried about my friends who are facing this pandemic away from the only home they have ever known.

The artwork on this square of toilet paper is the view from Mussolini's balcony, where fascism was born. I spent six months in Italy drawing and painting fascist architecture in 2018. Now I bring you this rendition of the view from Mussolini's balcony on a square of toilet paper. for your viewing and contemplative pleasure.

Art and Entertainment are an extremely important part of my life, during the good and specially the scary times.

Film, art and babysat with sewing projects as a child, at nine, I learned English watching "Married with Children."

My parents used art supplies, books and movies to reward and motivate me to be productive. This pandemic as we keep loosing countless lives, I'm looking forward to lying to my self about Captain Marval, when she brings back all the real life super s/heroes. I cried over losing all outhouse characters in Avengers Infinity Wars, knowing Captain Marvel would bring most of them back. Meanwhile Mango Mussolini is tearing down all of our political theater's backdrop with his Cheetos covered baby hands, and there is no comic book I can refer to in my mind that can undo all of his hate and greed. All my memories are comprised of what songs, artworks, textiles and film I was obsessed with at said time. During this Pandemic I feel like we are collectively binge watching a messed up timeline where the illusions of the cash economy are crashing, loss of life that can be stoped by a federal snap reaction is lacking and we are all sitting at home. We are feeling alone, while watching the worse writing playout as the political backdrop falls off and we see our corrupt "leaders" plugging up help for everyday people while letting the top 600 families, gut the resources meant for around 4,000,000 People.

I'm not unfamiliar with moments that require one to shutout life and do art alone at home. During this pandemic I'm reaching for my memories when and where after PTSD inducing times, I sit in solitude and art till I can build myself back up to feeling like a person again.
In 2009 my parter of 20 years and I were kidnaped in Iran. For three years I didn't go outside, I sat at home and drew, wrote, sewed, and arted alone till I felt safe again. In 2015 I had four brain surgeries, my ICU room was always full of friends and family. Having people with me in the ICU during the two months when I had four brain surgeries is the only way I made it out okay. I would have literally died if I had to be alone in the hospital for two months. Dying alone is the worse thing in the multiverse and it's currently happening to countless people. In 2017, the Muslim Ban deported my uncle and my family was threatened. I survived throughout my ordeals by hiding

and arting alone at home. One of my greatest joy has been filming a movie with a friend and the camera my mom bought us. As a conceptual artist, I am fascinated with sculpting new genres for film using different media, such as lighting, projection, sound, and recycled materials. I make instillation art like the sets I used to build as a kid and perform in.

My passion has always been in story telling, cinematography, set design, painting a story into life, sculpting it or sewing a character into resistance. When the impossible to deal with knocks on my door, I turned to Art.

My art has taken me to great highs like curating over 67 feminist artists at MOCA Tehran, in 2007. Which continues to be their largest attended and feminist exhibition to date. Which also had me arrested. In 2009 I went back to curate solo shows for all the artists featured in our MOCA Tehran Exhibition. Staring with master painter Masami Teraoka's epic water color paintings. Created for and about Japan in the 1970. Which was perfect for Iran during the green revolution of 2009. It got me blindfolded, hooded, kidnapped and nearly raped and murdered. But when I got away by the skin locked between my jaws, I curated that exhibition. (I find planed art time to be too tame. I enjoy being my creative practice's bitch. It takes me to more interesting places).

After graduating from Otis, I packed four suitcases, two carry-ons and a computer bag full of art, and traveled to MOCA Tehran in 2007 to curate "Manifestation of

Contemporary Arts in Iran." The exhibition featured works from 67 Iranian and American artists, including Suzanne Lacy, Masami Teraoka, Jerri Allyn, and Bill Viola. In 2015, I overcame four Brain Surgeries, and it was the movies, films and my favorite TV shows and series that brought me back to life yet again. The multiverse of Motion pictures, has not only shaped my existence. These families of glowing characters on screen have helped me build myself, the light and joy in me, back up after each time I've fallen ill or on hard times.
I believe in humanity,

We are all gonna come together!

This pandemic is just Mother Earth giving us a timeout. Our collective reflection on our ways, is bound to create positive changes. Post pandemic we'll have a clear chart of which leaders work for their people and which governments dang even pull their heads outa their corruption, enough to save lives in need of breath.

Which governments are lending their people's lungs ventilators and air versus which "leaders" are using these pandemic times to divide up our planet earth's resources while people are too busy dying alone to notice.

Website: http://www.MarjanV.com

Remembering:
Mother, Mansoureh Kheyabani Homaie, March 5th, 2021, Tehran Iran

Monica Marks

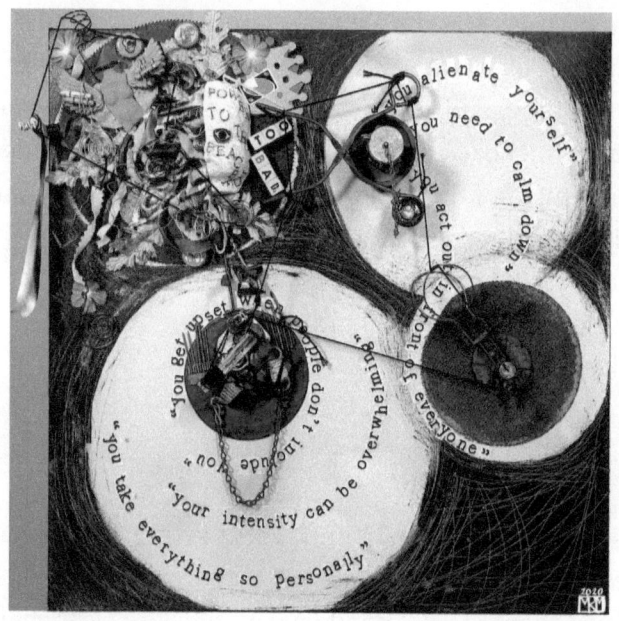

Name: Monica Marks
Discipline: Artist
Country: United States of America

2020:
I think extroverts are basically emotional vampires. I base this on something my mom has often told me, that the difference between introverts and extroverts is that the former gets energized by alone time and the latter gets energized by social time. Conversely, introverts are drained by "peopling," and extroverts are drained by isolation. So when introverts feel drained, they recede back into their safe, small places; when extroverts feel drained, they go find people and, if they find an introvert, they

suck the life force out of them. It's a survival instinct, nothing personal, really.

I am an introvert and many of the people in my family, some of whom I work with, are extroverts. Most of the other people at work are extroverts, too, except for the ones in my department, since we are all art therapists and so, by the stereotypical nature of our profession, we are all introverts. My experience is that extroverts tend to behave like recently converted religious fanatics, pyramid scheme salespeople, attendees at a motivational TedTalk who now view themselves as everyone's all-knowing Life Coaches. These are the ones who complain about introvert behavior and tell me I should "speak up more," "talk louder," "be more social," "loosen up…" —you know, be more like them. For the record, I have never, no matter how much I wanted to, told an extrovert they really should shut up more often.

Throughout my life I have been bullied for things that, I now realize, are simply the traits of introverts. These bullying acts are sometimes overt, sometimes microaggressions, or sometimes just leaving me out of something because I'm "no fun." It all came to head one day in an intense and heated call with a family member who proceeded to provide me with a list of all the things I do wrong that end up making people avoid me. I wrote down this list on a piece of scrap paper, things like; "You alienate yourself," "you take everything so personally," and, "your intensity can be overwhelming."

The energy it takes to try to "pass" as the average, well-adjusted person, one without social anxiety or the traits of an empath, is exhausting. I'm constantly searching for social cues and the correct replies, I'm always dampening the giddy excitement I have at the smallest things, and I'm forever faking some shell of an outgoing, confident, and self-assured human that I'm simply not. So, not only do I have to be around people (which is already draining in and of itself), but I have to try to be a version of a human they would feel comfortable around and accept. I try, but I'm not good at not being me.

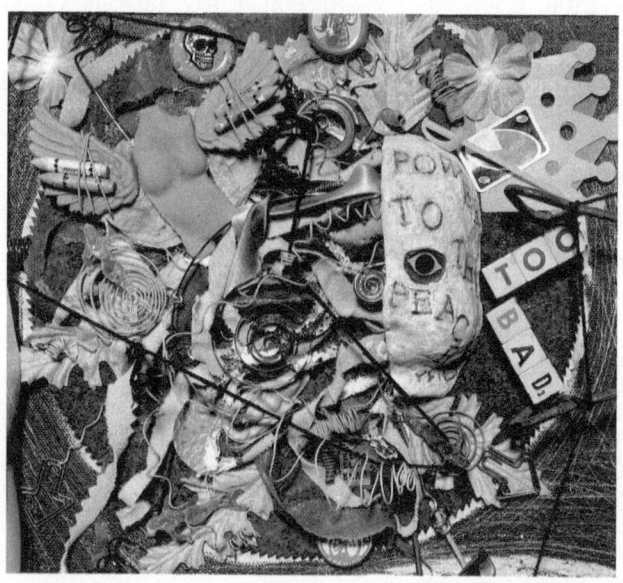

I stomped around my little art studio (where this call took place) hurt and fuming. The words I had written down were still running through my head, but carried the weight of all the other hurtful "constructive criticism" I had been subjected to throughout my life. I grabbed a canvas.

I was motivated to use something I never used before, something that would show the intensity they complained about, so I sprayed the canvas with fluorescent spray paint. Then I covered most of the canvas in black, leaving four distinct circles of color, representing the four us in my family. I went back with a scratching tool, furiously scratching the surface, each stroke fueled by the anger that I had kept under wraps for so long.

I started with the circle that represented me, continuing with the intense colors of my inner world pouring and exploding out of the open side of half a doll head. Fluorescent bursts of wire and clay and paper, found objects and ribbon, playing cards and dolls, bottle caps and buttons, were a passionate display of screaming colors that were finally allowed to flow free.

I kept coming back to it, piecing together representations of the other three family members. Around those I added the "helpful list" that I had since typed up and printed out, cutting out each letter so that the words would swirl around my symbolic family like painful fragments of an argument you can still feel hanging in the air after it's long over.

I used string to attach all the elements as they interconnect in my life. My verbal response to all the critics were spelled out in game tiles and became the title of this piece: TOO BAD.

This piece was a turning point for me this year, a moment in which I stopped apologizing for myself, for being an introvert, for being intense and creative and sensitive, where I stopped apologizing for being me.

Take that, vampires.

Website: https://www.monicamarksart.com/

Christianna Soumakis

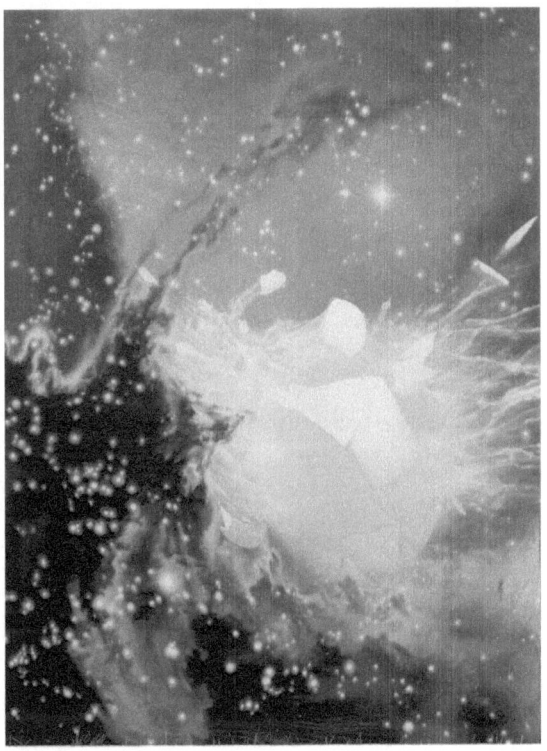

Name: Christianna Soumakis
Discipline: Artist
Country: United States of America

2020:
The Oral Defense
Christianna Soumakis

In the green room that used to be my sister's, I'm preparing to give the oral defense on which my graduate degree depends.

It's been four years since I began a low-residency Master of Fine Arts degree. Twice a year I fly from New York to LA to join my cohort and present my projects to mentors and peers for feedback, guidance, and grading.

The trip to Cali has always felt like part of the academic experience, a "higher time" when I've put my work and life on hold to fly into a different climate and context. I become a student, a creature on a track towards a goal, an ascendant thing, bound upward. I bumble out of LAX and drag myself and my luggage to campus, ensconce myself in whatever living arrangements I've been assigned, and let the syllabus accelerate me into the semester.

My cohort and I have been preparing for our 2020 Senior Thesis Shows all year. I've been cranking out paintings and performances and writing pieces and installations, writing proposals for gallery spaces, and deliberating on what I should wear to my thesis show's opening night for a stupidly long time.

I've imagined my opening, and my oral defense, a million times. The gallery's white walls, the shadowless lighting, bodies crushed in the space, the patchwork of voices ravelling and unravelling. I imagined myself, in some meticulously calculated outfit in which I look both careless and elegant, working the room, reading it, absorbing and redirecting the energy like a windsurfer of attention. Childlishly and with relish I imagined my resounding success, the approval of everyone I respected. Like a groomless wedding, I muse. How marvelous.

And here we are. Here we are, at last, on the day of my defense. All the work is done, all the effort is over, and I have only this last hurdle before I can collect my diploma and march into the world with my degree.

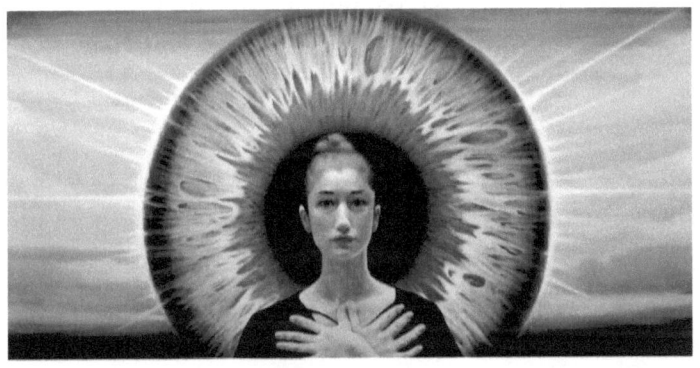

Here I am, not in a gallery, but in my sister's old bedroom, in New York, with my laptop open as I wait for the host to start the meeting. Here I am alone in my parent's house, where we have been quarantining these past few months, where we all had Covid-19 together in March, where I have to use the green room because my own room never has service. Here I am, a thirty-three-year-old adult living with Mom and Dad, having moved the paintings I worked on all year into the attic. Waiting for whatever is going to happen after quarantine. Waiting to find out if there will ever be an "after quarantine." Waiting to figure out what to do next, waiting for Amazon to ship me some courage — they seem to be helplessly backlogged — so I can figure out what I will actually do with an art degree in a world without jobs. Waiting for the host to start the meeting.

Breathe, I command myself. This is not the time for doom-and-gloom negativity. I check my body for an emotional status report: giddy, nervous, excited. I've always been a talker. I've even been told I should do stand-up. So unlike most of my peers, I've been really looking forward to some academic bantering; I'm sure I can hold my own. Beneath the tiered strata of stress and stage fright seeps the assurance that I will shine.

But I also feel like I'm a light that's been put under a bushel. The moment I've been preparing for feels like it's been pre-emptively stolen by a slippery, unprosecutable thief named Corona, and my anger and loss are without direction.

Zoom's civil white rectangle suddenly burps up a twirling circle, and the face of my program's director appears. I blink at him: this is happening. This is The Thing. I put my haters-come-at-me face on and make eye-contact with the central blackhead of my Mac's camera.

My laptop becomes a world of squares, and each square has a face, and this is how we are together. This is my room full of people. Part of my thesis was on the importance of the body in art and spiritual practices, how we so often are in danger of reducing and retracting life all the way up our spines, past our throats, into the front of our skulls "and slightly to the left" (to borrow Sir Kenneth Robinson's phrase) and live in that Cartesian, self-referencing hall of mirrors as though it were the whole world: disembodied, abstracted, objectified, cold. And here we are, in this brave bodiless new world: a crowd of two-dimensional heads, served on the platter of a screen that vanishes from my conscious attention as soon as it's turned on. A flock of squares has come to my oral defense. The thing I feared has come upon me.

My committee — the two mentors who have worked with me all year — open the discussion.

We have an hour. I know they'll question me for the first twenty minutes or so, and then the rest of the faculty will be invited to share criticisms, comments, and questions of their own.

My friend adrenalin has arrived, a hot flood of roaring through me, all surge and action, punchy language, big gestures. Boom. Words rush to my head like alcohol. My frontal lobes tapdance. I don't know what I sound like, but I feel like the cavalry in one of those Lord of the Rings battles, where they fly banners and blow trumpets and hurl themselves into the ranks of evil orcs (sorry, faculty!) with such unanswerable beauty and truth that the much larger force is overwhelmed by sheer virtue in a few minutes of screen time. (Later I watch the recorded Zoom footage, and I am sorry to report that although I was not denied a degree, I was also not a Legolas-Aragorn hybrid of chivalric victory. Reality is often disappointing.)

One of my favorite professors opens his remarks with: "You are a frenetic, scintillating square on my screen." Everyone laughs. I have a reputation for being a kind of human Red Bull, a small but powerful container of not entirely natural levels of energy. I am an intellectual Tigger: bouncey-flouncey-boucey-flouncey-fun-fun-fun-fun-fun, but make it academic. And so I careen through the barbed and pixelled Hundred Acre Wood of my online oral defense, always popping gamely back up when I land on my tail. (Maybe we can convince Peter Jackson to direct a LOTR sequel where Tigger leads the charge against the forces of Mordor? Pooh could be Frodo, Piglet could be Samwise, Eeyore could be Gimli… Sauron could be an outsized heffulump…?)

Five minutes from the end of my hour, another professor closes the meeting with some kind words. I have a suspicion everyone has been a little gentler than they might have been, given our current predicament. Maybe if I'd been there in person, without a global pandemic pumping us all full of empathy and a longing for human contact, the orcs would have taken Tigger down.

But there is no space for what-ifs. The meeting is over. The director says goodbye. He ends the meeting. My screen flips to the Zoom's post-meeting screen. And that's it.

That's the end. That's all. I did it. It's over. I'm alone in this green room, nothing between me and graduation, and whatever comes after that. No ceremony, no ritual to staunch the hemorraging wound of my educational career. Just the soft click of my closing laptop.

I put my hand on my tummy, like a kindergartener trying to self-regulate. I am a river after a flood: everything wet and limp and glistening, with a high water mark stamped far up the trunks of trees while the stream drains and drains until its bed is exposed. And all the secret rocks that were there the whole time come dark and shining into the light. And the water sinks lower and humbler, until everything dries and you can hike right down into the place where the white water would have killed you in seconds. And you can stand there in the quiet and the drought, and you can hear the wind softly blowing through this low, empty place, this place with everything scraped off it by a force that is now absent.

Where there was rushing and rumbling and crashing and pressure and violence and froth and spray, there is a dry road. You can stand still in the middle of this bald abandoned ribbon, you can stop charging and stop bouncing, and listen instead to your breath and your heartbeat and feel everything slowing, subsiding.

A deep hollow place, a canyon of pause, terrible and peaceful and lonely. A place gentle with loss. And the hawks circle high in the sky, and you can feel, can almost smell, the seasons changing as unhurriedly as they do — fearlessly, tirelessly, turning in and out of the light: the silent, slow, courageous, planetary march into the future.

Website: https://www.christiannasoumakis.com/artists

Simone Gad

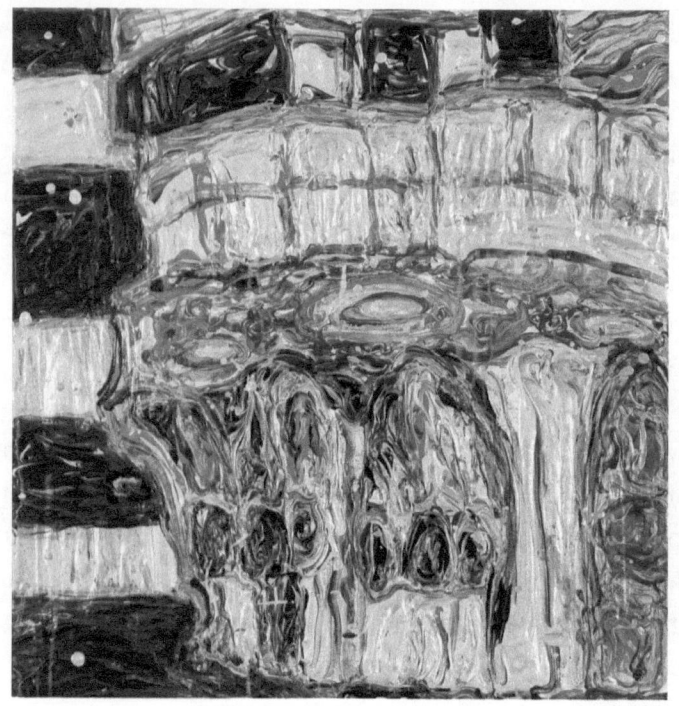

Name: Simone Gad — written January 4, 2021
(She is remembered. RIP February 25, 2021)
Discipline: visual artist
Country: Belgium born, US Citizen.

2020:
I had a colonoscopy June 10th 2020 and found out on the operating table as I was recovering from the procedure, when the surgeon informed me that I had a masticated giant tumor in my colon needing to be removed asap. I got a couple of very scary first opinions on my impending surgery and decided to go to another hospital to get a

second opinion where I had my first cancer surgery performed in 2015. When I got to the hospital for my appointment, I burst into tears, terrified. The surgeon assured me after looking at my colonoscopy photos I brought with me that I wouldn't need chemo aand radiation but that I'd need to be scheduled right away to have my surgery. A friend brought me on July 15th which had been my parents anniversary and my father's birthday, to get 4 Covid tests to make sure I was negative and then I was admitted into the hospital, had my surgery hours later, and spent 8 days recovering.

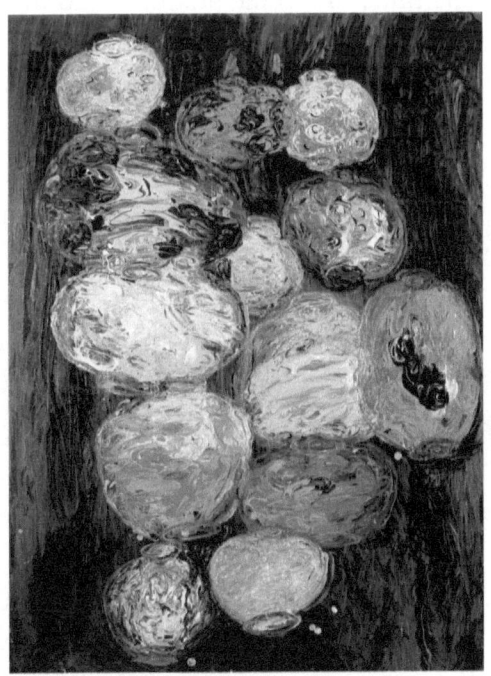

I had a pacemaker inserted into my upper chest soon after my colon cancer procedure and then was sent home. A week later I was called to Emergency, because my surgery was...something had gone wrong with it, and apparently, I had become sepsic. I waited for hours and was finally admitted again, but this time to the ICU where I was placed on a ventilator for 16 days, nearly not making it through alive. Subsequently, I had multiple surgeries and spent 3 months altogether in the hospital. Then I was sent to Rehab to relearn how to walk which took another 3 and a half weeks, my thinking I'd not make it home, though I was determined to, my constantly thinking of my elderly kitty Ashes who was waiting for me at home. My friend, Michael, took care of my apartment and my cat the whole time, the whole Summer, and then I finally was released, getting home on September 9th. I am still in recovery, but am able to make my art every day and am so very grateful to be alive. While in Rehab, I had a VAC machine attached to my stomach I had to schlep to the bathroom day and night and for the next 2 months after I got home. It was heavy to lug around, to say the least. On October 14th, the VAC machine was removed by my surgeon to my relief, my wounds having closed on my stomach. It took me several days to realize I didn't have to drag that machine around anymore. The wounds are closed, thankfully, but I have an ugly giant purple scar all the way up and down my stomach to my groin and a little ketone thing that needs to be lanced that leaks from time to time. Not a big leak, but it's icky and constantly needs to be watched by the RN who comes over now once a week to dress it. As it turns out, I don't need to have chemo and radiation do to my age and also because the masticated tumor hadn't spread to other parts of my body. I am so damn lucky. My parents passed away many years ago. They were holocaust survivors living in L.A. My brother too passed away at the age of 39. I thought of my family the whole time I was in the hospital, and I also thought of my cat, non-stop. She was the goal for me to make it through and it worked. She clings to me day and night and sleeps on my bed for hours and hours and she too is my nurse who saved my life.

Website:
https://www.track16.com/simone_gad_architecture_acide

Cindy Zimmerman

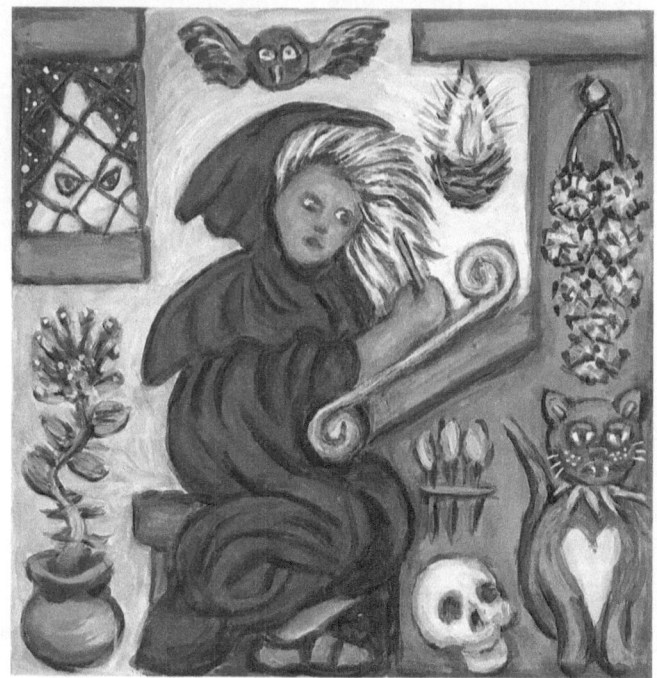

Name: Cindy Zimmerman
Discipline: Visual Art
Country: United States of America

2020:
Spring 2020 was wide open for possibility. I had ended my last contract as an Adjunct Professor in Fall 2019. My last formal teaching assignment was Introduction to Art at Richard J. Donovan Correctional Facility, on behalf of Southwestern College. I loved this job but was time for a change.

I started the New Year with an artist residency at Desert Dairy in 29 Palms; to get the solitude I craved, look at where I had been and where I was going, and to stoke some small fires in my imagination. But then the pandemic hit. Like all of us, I experienced a lot of emotions and cognitive dissonance. I was making art intermittently with obsessing on the news, crying, reaching out to friends and family, looking for whatever equilibrium I could find.

My daughter-in-law and son were expecting a child, and filled with worries about what was to come. They were lucky that she could take time off from work, and he (also an Adjunct Professor) was already good at teaching remotely. Their other two boys had the technology, support and space for their studies, too.

But my kids couldn't figure out how to safely birth the baby, given their stringent standards for safety from contagion. We had been distancing, masking, and limiting ourselves to occasional backyard visits and, through our conversations, I hit on the idea of quarantining myself for a month or two around the time the baby would be born. My husband, John, was too out-in-the-world for safety, keeping our nonprofit circus running, and leading the performers in popup performances around food distribution lines.

So I rented an Airbnb near our little apartment and moved in. Solitude with a twist!

My husband could bring me groceries and anything I needed from home. After a few days, I figured out that a small craft table and my super small bottles of acrylic paint could fit in a corner of the alcove off the bathroom, with my reading light and some window light mixing in a lovely way.

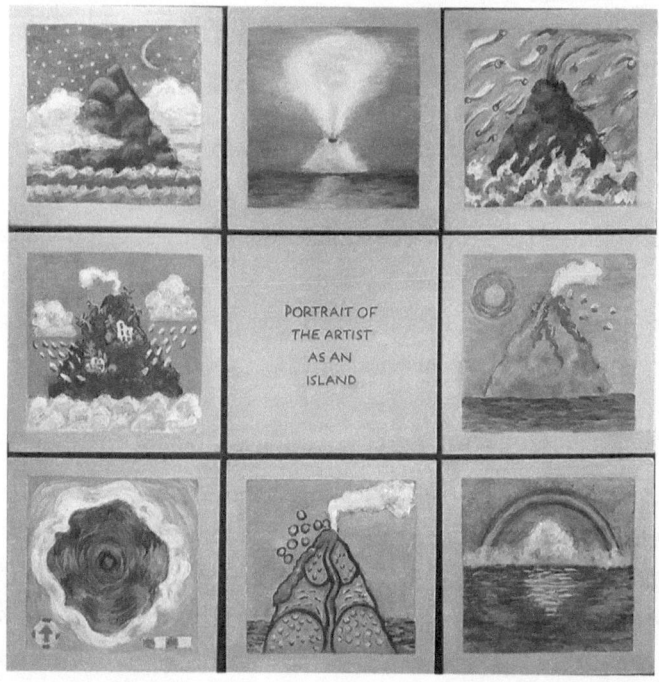

There was a cooking area, minus a stove, but with a microwave, toaster oven, sink, and a glass-topped table for eating. That table was a great place to lay out the little paintings-on-panel that I was making, so I could see them together.

Besides painting, I read plague literature, including Parable of the Sower (Octavia Butler), Station 11 (Emily St. John Mandel), World War Z (Max Brooks), The End of October (Lawrence Wright) and The Stand (Stephen King).

My host lived in the main house, and we made small talk when I went out for walks in the neighborhood. I hardly went anywhere else, and the battery on my car died so hard that it had to be replaced.

John and I are very close, so we developed the habit of having dinner together every night, sitting outside behind my lodging, at the recommended distance. We even bought new camping chairs to enhance the experience. I would heat up the food he had bought for me, and place it on a little table where he could pick it up, masked, and get back to his chair without breathing on me.

I figured out that we could touch, feet to feet, while still maintaining the 6' requirement, and he was willing to indulge my idea. We used a cardboard box to make it less tiring.

Every day, I painted. My paintings are autobiographical, and informed by my upbringing in the Catholic religion. Mostly a combination of profane and sacred, they are my own unauthorized version of spiritual experience. They also include a concern for the collective good, as the radical clergy who shaped my conscience in the 1950s and 60s taught me.

I am the oldest of eight sisters, and my childhood was organized around the need to help sustain the family. Over the years, I have learned that what I want and need most of all is solitude. But I need affiliation too, so I have cycled between the two. This quarantine stay was right in line with experiences I have sought out my whole life.

I had the virtue of being of service to my family, with the pleasure of doing what I wanted when I wanted, with no one looking over me, or monitoring my condition. I could be sad, confused, purposeful or ecstatic, in the moment or out of it.

While I painted, I thought sometimes about being over seventy years old, and whether I might die. What would I want to leave behind? What do I see from this vantage point that I might want to express, and in a way that was not necessarily comfortable for me? I was able to take more time. I returned again and again to trying to get it right. I needed some new iconography. I risked branching out in genres.

When the kids called, ready to go to the hospital, I dropped everything, packed up a little bag, and stayed with the big boys for a few nights until mom and dad could come home. A few days later, I was back at the Airbnb, so I could be on standby in case they needed me.

When the stay was over, and I moved back in to my bubble with John, I had this new work to look at and think about. Not sure yet how it integrates, and I haven't exactly made it into a continuity. My output has always been intermittent, and at this point, I am past career building. I like to tell myself that by now, the work I make is just between me and god--lower case--as I understand god.

Mostly, I just follow my visions, and my inner voice, and take it one day at a time. With my art and with my life right now, like Baby Ben, I am trying to stay open to possibility.

Website: http://www.cindyzimmerman.work

Our Ever Changing World: Through the Eyes of Artists: Book 14

Stuart Rapeport

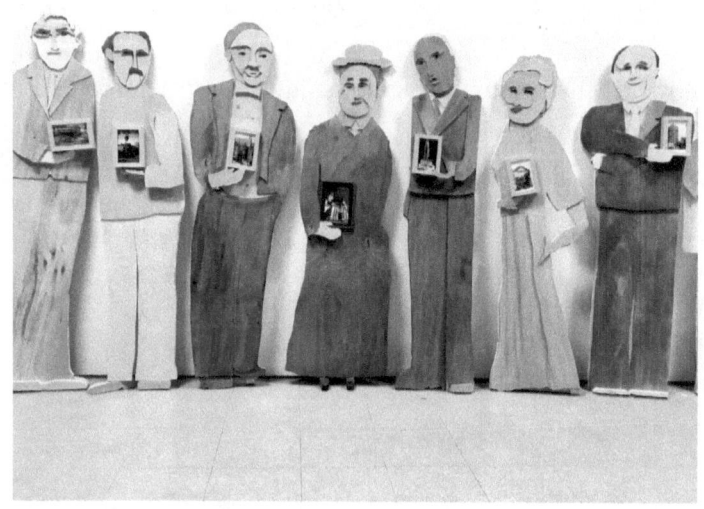

Name: Stuart Rapeport
Discipline: art and stuff
Country: United States of America

Focus Year 2020
what's next?

When 2019 ended there was optimism for 2020. My work was included in a major exhibit acknowledging the importance of Walter Hobbs.

The Art Peeps found a comfortable venue at the Yucca Valley Art Center. and made a good fit in honoring Walter Hobbs. The installation was well receieved by those that were able to find their way to Yucca Valley on the road to

Joshua Tree. A well known art critic drove out to the venue only to find it closed. It had closed for the Thanksgiving week. Who knew? A few weeks later more of the Art Peeps, representing the people involved in the Los Angeles art world. were invited to be installed at West Los Angeles College. A few friends drove to the campus and it was closed for the winter break. They would have to take my word for it how cool the installation looked.

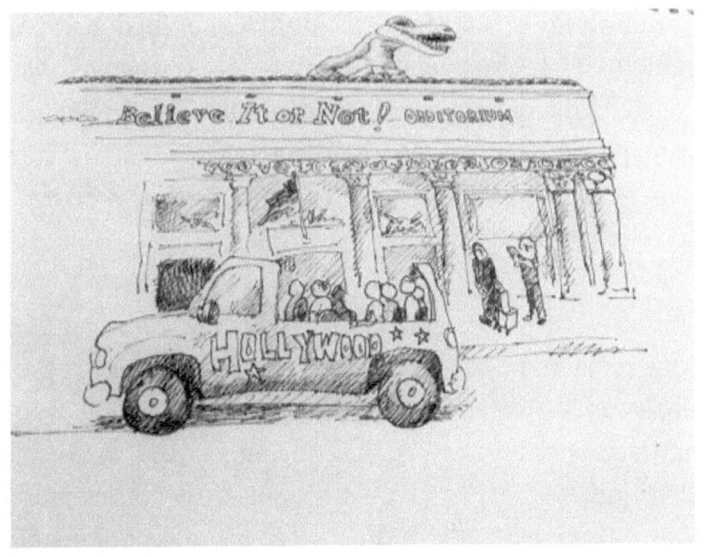

2020 began optimistically. The Hollywood Heritage and Preservation group was exhibiting a model of 1940's Hollywood neighborhood in their venue on Hollywood Boulevard. I was invited to create images of the architects that were the influencers and builders of Hollywood. They would be placed areound the model, admiring the models of their work. A dozen figures were created. The show opened , it looked fine. Cyclavia did one of their bike rides down the boule-vard, thousands a people rode by. The work was going to be seen. The work wasn't abour sales but interacting with people. There would be lots of people.

About a week later there was a George Floyd protest and the boulevard was shut down. Store-fronts were boarded up after some buildings had windows broken. A month went by and the first news of the Covid-19 flu was spreading. Tourism stopped. Hollywood Blvd had less traffic than the highway to Joshua Tree. Businesses were slow to come back and attract the public. The Presidential primary election was about to happen and many store owners decided it was safer to keep the stores boarded up. The pandemic was getting worse.

The resturants, bars and other Hollywood tourist attractions remained closed. For lease signs were going up on what was just recently souvineer shops. The Hollywood Heritage and Pres-ervation venue remained closed and the windows covered with plywood. The tourist buses were disappearing, the people street was absent of people. Inside the boarded up building was a really fun exhibit, a model of old Hollywood and Rudolf Schindler was discussing his work with Richard Neutra, Frank Lloyd Wright was keep his eyes on the development. Julia Morgan and Paul Williams were comparing notes. Lou Naidorf was bragging about the Columbia Records. Mary Pickford. Paul DeLongpre, Daeidra Wilcox, admir-ing how the small town had exploded with development.

The installation remains boarded up, so you need to take my word for how cool it looks.

Maybe it will open up again soon, but hard to imagine Hollywood Boulevard will be coming back to the energized street that it was a few months ago. maybe it will.

Hopefully a new President that takes its role in disaster preparation seriously will find a way to get the city energized again…maybe?

Website: http://www.rapeport.com

Our Ever Changing World: Through the Eyes of Artists: Book 14

Malado Francine Baldwin

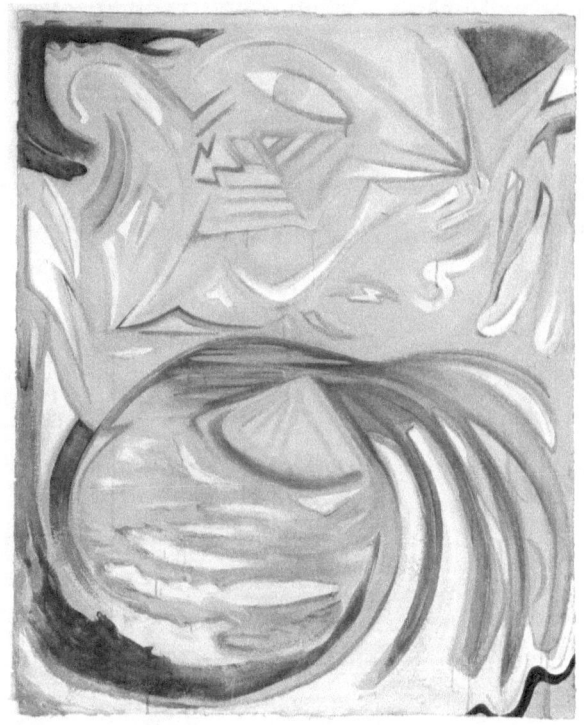

Name: Malado Francine Baldwin
Discipline: Visual Arts (Painting, Film, Sculpture)
Country: United States of America

2020:
*Advice to a young neighbor girl
by Malado Francine Baldwin

My living room, to be precise, is serving as a studio during Covid, and I'm bursting at the seams with projects and eager to get them out in the world. They line the walls for my only visitor. The cards I pull keep saying: Patience. Signs..... But all this making, and more making, during this pandemic- it's the first time, I've had, literally, so much time.

Athena, almost ten, lives next door and stops by often. She asks me many questions and also praises and flatters me constantly. This is AMAZING. How do you do all this? (I don't know, it just comes to me). How long did it take? (It depends, for this one, it started out as a journal, I took a photo of the page, I projected it and made a pencil sketch, then painted, adding details and changing things). -How long, though? (Maybe a few weeks, months? Even, to be more precise, possibly years?) Do you make art everyday? (Most days, in some or several forms, yes). (What I didn't say: It insulates me from the world, like building a nest of visions —I am that crow with her shiny objects lining her view: who will visit and be impressed?)

Wow, so Amazing, she says, with emphasis on AMAZING.

What I didn't tell her, but will, when she is older~ about inspiration and art and why I never get bored or run out of things to make- is to somehow find a way to live a non-predictable life... to have something to brag about, (even ridiculous or disastrous), as endeavors make for good stories when told right, with a sense of self-ridicule, and gratefulness. And they feed you, constantly, with options and ideas and inspirations for more.

....Like that trip to Ghana with Felix and Gracie and Will, taking public buses on dirt roads from Mali to Burkina Faso to Ghana, and back. Rebels at the border in Burkina, sleeping in ditch, bus on fire and border checks. The boys got fleas and we all lost weight, but at least Gracie and I got a seat. The boys stood in the aisles with the sheep and chickens, the dust and bags, keeping steady eyes on the road ahead.

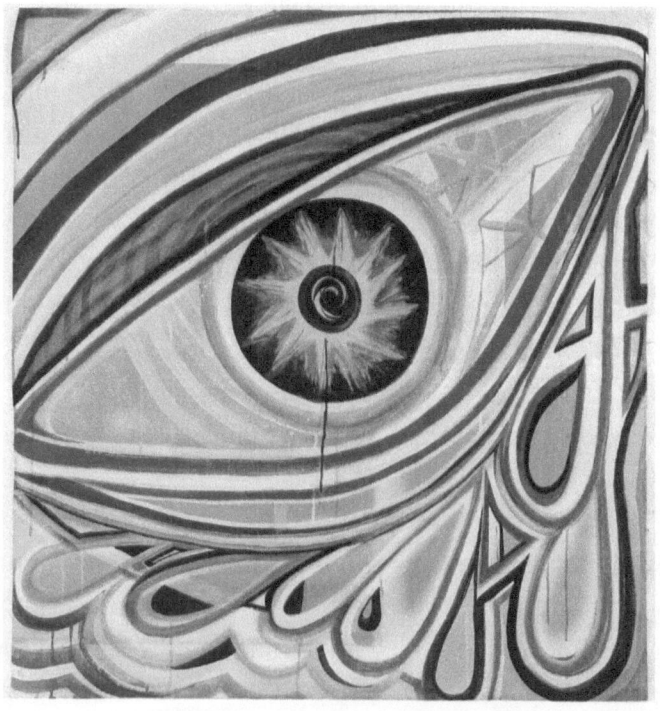

And then the shocks blew on our trip to Timbuktu. But we were there, in a sandstorm in the vast Sahara~ despite it all. And after, the requisite sunset camel ride and Moroccan mint tea in the dunes with photos to prove it was true. We spent a glorious New Year's Eve in a tiny club, dancing to Tuareg music, with Gracie and Alexandra and the local girls, their heads covered, teaching us their delicate arm moves, more beautiful than I'd ever seen (and moves I still use).

We came back dusty, discovered, wide-eyed: I'd just introduced three Americans to Africa — I think it blew their minds.

I'd tell her, this Athena, who comes over more and more as her world shrinks with Covid restrictions- I'd tell her, keep that ravenous appetite and keep replenishing it, feed your desire to know and experience and meet and greet the new; your neighbor, your neighboring continent, your unknown next stop- with wonder. Witness and just keep asking those great questions, my dear new friend.

Thank you, my biggest-smallest fan.

Website: http://www.maladofrancine.com

Barbara Fritsche

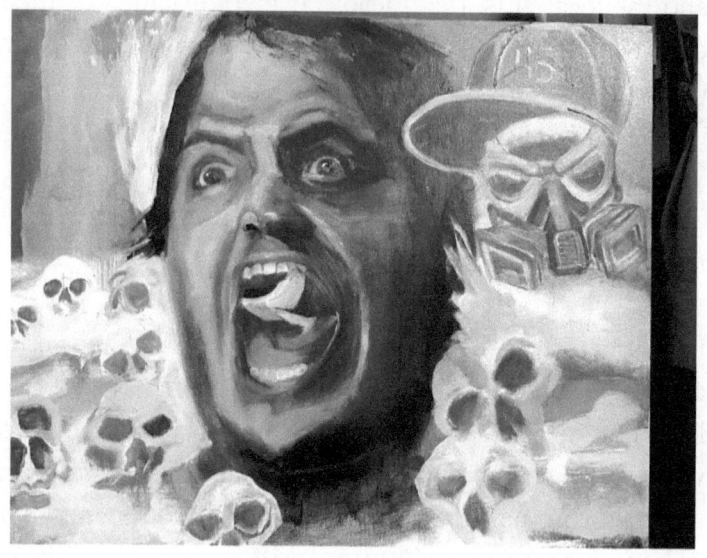

Name: Barbara Fritsche
Discipline: Artist
Country: United States of America

2020:
2020 my passions closed, shut down then again I'm an artist Happy to be a painter. It calls into my life those parts of my mind which direct both eye and hand. Light and color-the truth of the beauty of line and form-I think this heightened sense of observation of nature is one of the chief delights that have come to me through painting.

Painting is a companion with whom one may hope to walk a great part of life's journey.

Age cannot wither her nor custom stake Her infinite variety!

My current works address the surreal, intangible world of social media, addictions, memories, dreams, and relationships, embracing the beautiful, bizarre, and melancholic. Driven to produce meditations on life, both from a real-time perspective, and a time lapse notion, a slice of everyday existence that brings to a head the trials of life as we know it.

COVID is challenging the human race like nothing else. On the positive side, air pollution is dropping, more than ever- nature is benefiting. I started walking in the neighborhood and local nearby parks one called Arroyo Verde located in Ventura, California photographing nature, specifically blooming flowers, they are exploding with breathtaking color and energy, giving visuals, one can smell, so inspiring, happy to paint nature's delights. The beauty of nature then starts to decline in a couple months the color is starting to change as the season progresses Yet as the pandemic grows and mankind struggles to understand how it spreads, the infrastructure is deemed a culprit and lock-downs go into effect, stay at home orders are given, to slow down the spread of this virus, an alarming number of humans around the world are getting sick, and the numbers of deaths are multiplying.

Many countries are struggling to find masks and supplies. In early February I started calling Hospital's in the Ventura area and discovered the scary truth that we are not prepared at this point only to recognize the seriousness of what's to come.

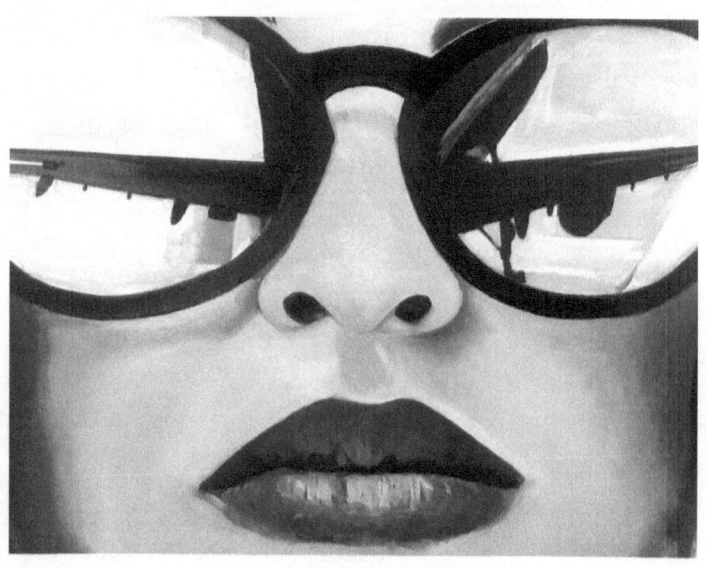

In my world of being a colorist the governor of California decided to close salons...there goes my bread and butter ...months into the shut down then my precious cat Chloe dies ..I wanted to scream and scream so I painted.

If existence is but a card game, is a moment of decision an eternity in the blink of an eye?

Website: http://www.barbarafritsche.com

Remembered:
Van Arno, 18/01/2021, Ventura, CA

Disha Dua

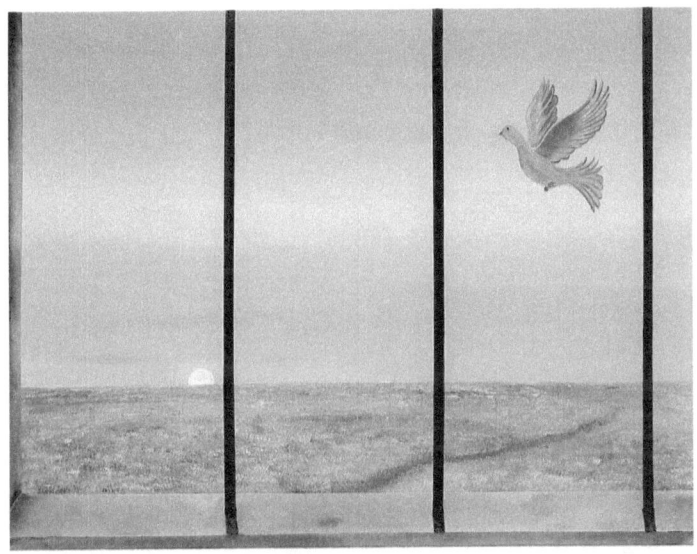

Name: Disha Dua
Discipline: Artist - Painting
Country: United States of America

2020:
Who is in the Cage?
Acrylics on Canvas, 36"W x 24"H

2020 has been an unprecedented year. It came with unforeseen challenges and valuable lessons. While we humans were locked down at home, I saw remarkable images of animals walking freely through deserted cities - ducks and dolphins reappearing in canals and nearing shores, birds settling in gardens, butterflies flying undisturbed, and plants growing in the cracks of empty streets.

And then it hit me, the tables had turned—our fortresses had transformed into cages. Humans Locked Down; Nature Unlocked.

A renowned Indian lyricist, poet and author, Gulzar, penned the below lines in his inimitable poetic style. His poetry resonated with me and inspired me to capture the sentiment in an artwork.

एक मुद्दत से आरज़ू थी फ़ुरसत की
    longed for leisure time,

मिली तो इस शर्त से कि किसी से न मिलो ।
    was granted to me, granted I don't meet anyone.

शहरों का यूँ वीरान होना कुछ यूँ ग़ज़ब कर गयी
    cities had such an effect

बरसों से पड़े गुम सुम घरों को आबाद कर गयी ।
    that lay quiet for years, started chirping again.

यह कैसा समय आया कि
    a strange time this is

दूरियाँ ही दवा बन गयी ।
    distance has become a survival drug.

ज़िंदगी में पहली बार ऐसा वक़्त आया
    unprecedented times

कि इंसान नें जिन्दा रहने के लिये कमाना ही छोड दिया ।
gave up their livelihoods to stay alive.

घर गुल्ज़ार   सूने शहर
Homes, isolated cities

बस्ती में कैद हर हस्ती हो गयी ।
being caged by its own creation.

आज फिर ज़िंदगी महंगी
again life was precious

और दौलत सस्ती हो गयी ।
money lost its allure.

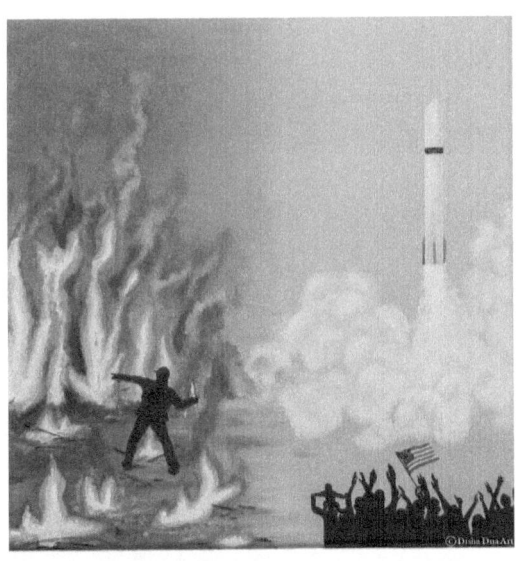

"USA, May 30th, 2020 - A tale of two fires". Description: May 30th, 2020, USA, a day of striking contrasts - a major milestone for space travel and the beginning of riots in major cities.

In July 2020, this artwork broke geographical barriers and made the cover-art for a song by an Estonia based music band. The song is called 'This is your life' by Lumm and was inspired by the current world crisis and mostly by the reaction of people to the new status quo.

Disha Dua Art
www.dishadua.com
Facebook: @DishaDuaArt
Instagram: @DishaDuaArt

Stevie Love

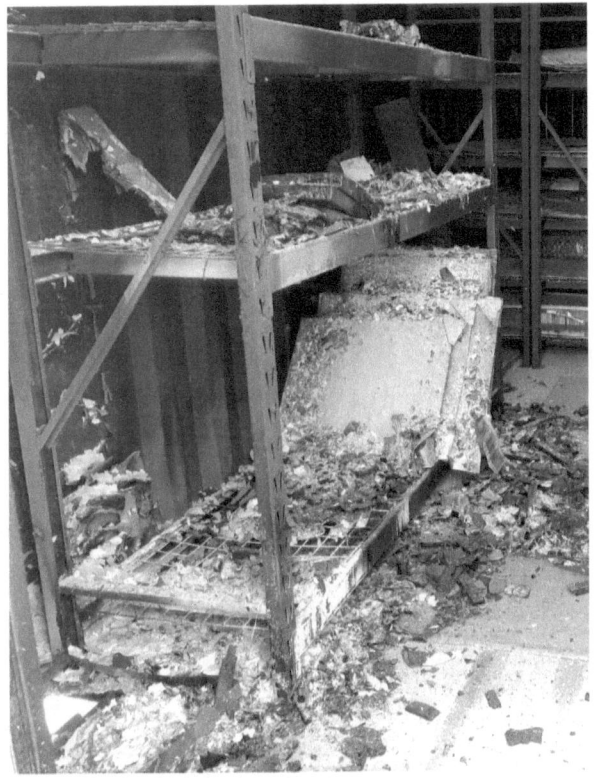

Name: Stevie Love
Discipline: Painting
Country: United States of America

2020:
Trial by Fire
Stevie Love

We saw the fire developing on the other side of the mountain in news reports, never thinking it would come this far. Surely it would be contained. Then it wasn't contained. Surely it would not jump Highway 2, then it did. A day later we saw smoke billowing into the sky east of us so we got in our four-wheel vehicle and drove the five miles to the top of the loop to see if we could see anything. Holy crap. There it was. Flames fifty feet high just over the ridge. Our hearts sank to see a house nestled high into the hillside.

Still, the fire was so far to the east, and now that it was moving into a neighborhood, surely it would be stopped before it got much farther. Of course, dear reader, you can see where this is going. That same day we had to evacuate. As we prepared to leave, bulldozers were cutting forty-foot wide swathes through the chaparral, planes roared close overhead dumping fire retardant in great red bands, and emergency vehicles, bulldozers on trailers, water trucks were everywhere.

As we drove off the hillside on the one paved road out of our neighborhood, we were stopped by a sherriff's deputy who wrote down our address as evacuated – one less house to be concerned whether there were people inside. With our dog and cat and not much else our friends welcomed us into their house in town out of harm's way.

In the next two days, Bruce made multiple scouting trips, avoiding the road blocks by using his knowledge of back roads navigable with four wheel drive. At one point he ran into a neighbor at a roadblock who was frantic to get home but when Bruce brought him up the hill the back way the flames and smoke were too thick to get to his house. Another time Bruce got within a quarter mile of our house and saw flames between him and the house, but the smoke was too thick to see if our house was still standing.

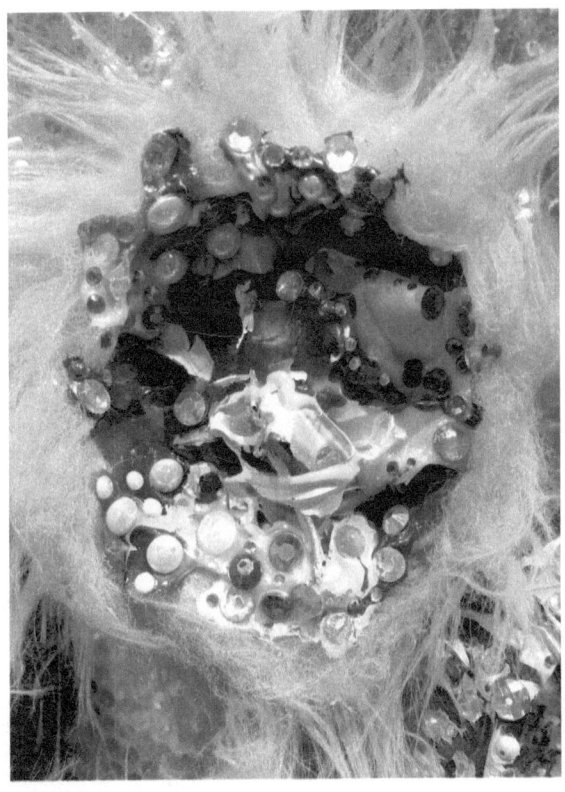

Two days later, the fire had moved through, and our neighbor on his quad had scouted the neighborhood and reported that our house was still standing so we decided to take the animals and move back. The roadblocks were still up so we navigated the back canyon. Sure enough the house looked untouched. The fire had burned everything within 50 feet of the house, 360 degrees. The hillside was a moonscape with gnarled black skeletons where huge trees had been.

As we drove in I noticed my 20-ft metal storage container where I stored artwork was still standing, but there were brownish smoke trails around the vent at the top corner.

After we checked inside the house, which looked just as we left it and it didn't even smell of smoke, I walked down to the storage container. As I got close, I could see that one of the railroad ties it was sitting on had burned so that the whole huge container was tipped slightly to one side, and the metal doors looked smokey. I opened the doors.

I had purchased that container three years earlier because my in-home studio was so stacked with twenty years of work that I had nowhere left to work. Bruce had made a nice level pad with his Bobcat, and the company from Fontana delivered the container and set it on two railroad ties that we had placed there for that purpose. I purchased some very sturdy steel shelving from Costco that went together with a rubber mallet. Really strong and practical.

I was so pleased moving all my work into that space, organizing as I went — I'd never been so organized. Boxes with smaller works had pictures on the outside of what was in the box. All the bigger paintings were protected by heavy plastic sheeting. The larger Paint Objects were labeled and rolled up on the shelves which I had doubled up to make four feet deep. I was a happy camper.

Then I opened the doors. That vision is seared into my brain. There is no other way to put it. Piles of ash on the steel shelves where artwork used to be. The bigger paintings on heavy panels that were sitting on the floor and leaning against the wall were black and melted together. Rolled up Paint Objects were burnt and melted onto the steel shelves. The fire got inside through the wooden floor that caught fire sitting on the railroad ties which by the way are soaked in creosote — so very flammable. I see how it happened.

It has been months since the fire and I've completed one new large work that has given me temporary reprieve from grief. The second image is a detail, one of fifty-five paint, gems, and faux fur. I am given to understand that it was a Sacred Fire. I am the Phoenix but with slightly clipped wings. With a shift in focus. I don't want to stack up another eighty works. But I live and breathe color and form. It's all I see when I close my eyes, fabulous suggestive shapes that can never be fully realized but that pull on me with hope and desire. So without knowing where I am going, the work of color and form pulls me forward, for now.

Website: http://www.stevielove.com

Kaz Maslanka

Similar Triangles
Triangles of the same shape but different sizes

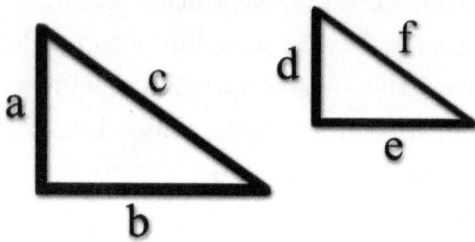

'a' is to 'b' as 'd' is to 'e'

Or synonymously speaking

$$\frac{a}{b} = \frac{d}{e}$$

$$\frac{\text{Freedom}}{\text{Money}} = \frac{\text{Obsession}}{\text{Irresponsibility}}$$

Name: Kaz Maslanka
Discipline: Mathematical Visual Poet
Country: United States of America

2020:
As a mathematical visual poet, I would like to share the inspiration that inspired my piece: "The Caveat of Capitalism—Freedom without responsibility is not free".

The year 2020 did not start in January—at least not for me. It started in February right after I purchased N95 masks for my Korean in-laws who flew back home from a vacation with my wife and me. The Coronavirus invaded planet earth like a cloaked invader appearing from another dimension and mysteriously picking off its victims one-by-one. It takes no effort to remember those days distinctly even though there was a dubious haze of disbelief when I realized that my universe was transformed into a B-rated science fiction movie. The virus was spreading across the world with fatal tragedies mounting, multiplying, and manifesting throughout major cities everywhere. Horror stories were coming out of New York City culminating with the dead being put in refrigerated trucks serving as temporary morgues on the street. Our hearts went out yet, we were helpless, frustrated, and heart-broken for there was nothing anyone could do about it. Where I live in Southern California the weather was stereotypical perfection with cloudless blue skies and palm trees dancing in the soft ocean breeze. One could argue it was paradise except for the fact that in another dark dimension there was an invader set to kill thousands of people right here in the bright shining sun. The confluence of such placid beauty and such eroding evil colored the world such that it was hard to relax much less enjoy. Anxiety crept into every situation imaginable affecting everything from business to family and marriages. As Americans we needed someone to lead the charge against this invader but instead, we had a president immersed in yes-men who denied its severity, pointed blame at others and initially charged that it was a political conspiracy. I believed that the leadership was well over their head, treading water and tried to cover their tracks up focusing on an easier target. Since the president was supposedly a businessman the spotlight illuminated the fiscal malady experienced by almost everyone. Thus, a conflict of values between the importance of financial hardship experienced by the many versus a few people experiencing horrible death in solitude while their families were wringing their hands, disconnected in disparate spaces outside of the hospital. This conflict of culture values was created, politicized, and sold to the American public for billions of dollars in media revenue. The response of the United States government was troubling at best and an act of selfish incompetency at worse. Yet, the problem was much worse than the poor performance of an inept government—for the confluence of social media and capitalism-run-amok created a nightmare for which we have not awoken—and I suspect we will not wake for many years.

We have been told by many, that as a country, one of our biggest virtues is our freedom. Furthermore, we must fight everything and everyone to protect it. Yet, few understand the mechanics of how freedom works. Let's look at the concept that one person's freedom is another person's prison. It might be best to start with an example: Let's say that my ancestors wrote an ancient book that stated that your property and home belonged to me and my family. Furthermore, I had the right to remove you from the property, bulldoze your home and take the property for my own. My freedom demands that I execute this plan so that I can be free to enjoy the property and make it prosperous for my family. Yet my freedom to live on that property puts you into a mental prison for you will become obsessed with trying to take it back from me. And if you take it back from me, I will be in a mental prison trying to figure out how I can take this land back again. And on and on …

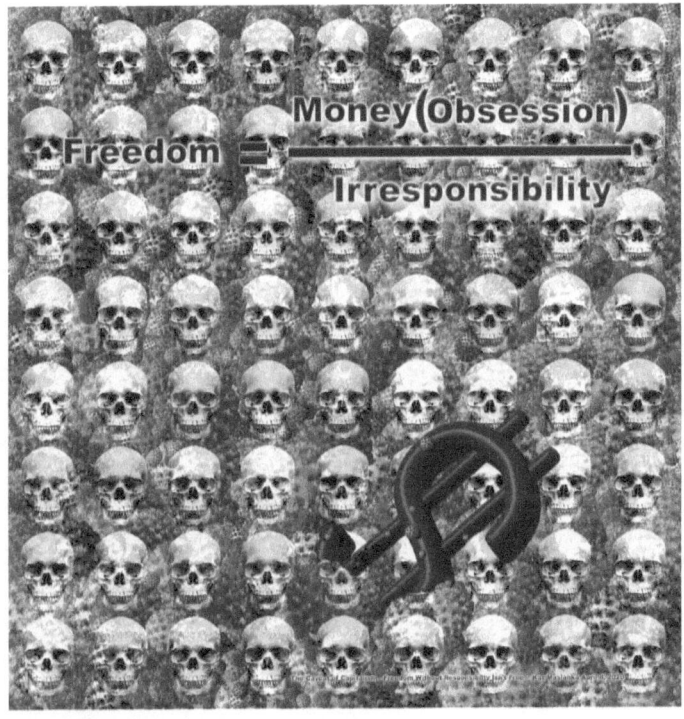

If the concept that 'one person's freedom is another person's prison' were embedded in the psyche of Americans then we would at least have some notion of tolerance concerning other people's freedom furthermore, we would understand that not everyone views of freedom are the same. In addition, we would also understand that it is 'cultural selfishness' that drives our particular belief in freedom no matter what it's definition is.—Before you jump to a conclusion of what I mean by cultural selfishness, let's talk about the core concept of culture. Within American society, there are countless cultures within cultures, within cultures or you may rather use the term subcultures or tribes. The cultures all differ but what all the members have in common is they all have the same beliefs and values. And since they all value their beliefs, you can create a concise definition for the 'nucleus of culture' to be a group of two or more people with the same values. It is the beliefs and values that define the culture. So it concludes that American society values disparate things with many of those values manifesting in different levels of conflict. The level of the conflict depends on how threatened one feels by the conflict. Since Americans in general value their freedom greatly, it is easy to see why the conflicts among freedom fighters are so intense. Furthermore, many people view their idea of Freedom to be American and anything opposing it as un-American. So it is easy to see conflict across the political spectrum manifesting in everything from trolling on social media to attacking Washington with an armed militia. No matter what side you are on, everyone in American society believes that their values are true 'American values', and those values that conflict with their own are a threat to the fabric of society. Therefore, we are all culturally selfish in that we believe that our values (not others) are the best for our great country. Furthermore, if others force their values upon me then I lose my freedom in the prison of their values. For they will chastise, denigrate, and restrict me from expressing my values. And if I force my values on them then they have lost their freedom In the prison of my values for I will chastise, denigrate and restrict them from expressing their values. Therefore, the concept of Freedom is not absolute—it is cultural and relative.

Freedom for any one person comes at a price no matter what their definition for it is. The definitions for freedom are complex but ostensibly, it doesn't mean "anything goes". For it is easy to see that an 'anything-goes' mentality is arguably selfish and irresponsible yet, so many Americans possess this destructive obsession. As all of our institutions became politicized, businesses failed, and COVID-19 deaths accumulated with conflicts of cultural values bubbling up to the surface of society quite early in the pandemic. Political rhetoric exacerbated the conflicts politicizing something that should never had been political. The conflict that inspired the piece shown in this introspection was human lives versus business and as an extension of business, the concept of money. Battles ensued among topics that included everything from wearing masks to being able to open the pandemically closed doors of businesses. The ideal of Freedom erected itself into the spotlights, promulgating the conflicts to the center of the stage for political partisan battles. Sadly, the values of generosity and altruism were never framed in such a way that they made their way into these conversations. In my frustration, I was inspired to create the mathematical visual poem titled: "The Caveat of Capitalism"- Freedom without Responsibility is not Free.

To fully appreciate the confluence of diverse disciplines, interdisciplinary expressions always requires some homework. While much art requires no foregrounding, mathematical visual poetry requires some basic algebra skills yet, more importantly an open willingness to understand how poetry is used in this way. It is beyond the scope of this paper to delve into the mechanics, cognitive linguistics and visual poetics involved in fully enjoying this piece. Yet, I have provided a link below that will fill in all of those blanks. I hope I have piqued your curiosity enough to study it further. That said, I will introduce this piece with the bare-bones approach while hoping that you will further investigate this form of poetics.

The piece shown here uses the same mathematical structure that is used to calculate the lengths of the legs in a pair of similar triangles. That is, 'a' is to 'b' as 'd' is to 'e' or in equation form as $a/b=d/e$. (See figure 1.) If we solve for 'a' then we get the form used in this poem: $a = b(d)/e$ or: Freedom = (money times obsession) divided by Irresponsibility.

In the vernacular; the mathematical poetic part of this expression can be read as such: "Freedom is to Money as Obsession is to Irresponsibility" or we can mathematically manipulate the syntax differently to read: "Freedom is to Obsession as Money is to Irresponsibility". The mathematics also expresses other concepts including the following: As the value of irresponsibility approaches zero the value of freedom approaches infinity. Or, as the value of money approaches zero the value of obsession approaches infinity. The visual elements in the piece include a substrate of coronaviruses underlying a layer of seventy-two tessellated human skulls. All these images are symbolically eroded by money.

Cognitive linguistics has given me the language to study and describe this mathematical visual poetic structure in detail. To understand mathematical visual poetry in general and similar triangles poems (like this one) in particular please read the paper "A Cognitive View of Pandemic Meditations" Published through the Film and Video Poetry Society in Los Angeles, California.
Also, it can be downloaded from this URL:
http://www.kazmaslanka.com/ACVOPM.html

Website: http://www.kazmaslanka.com

Our Ever Changing World: Through the Eyes of Artists: Book 14

Doug Eisenstark

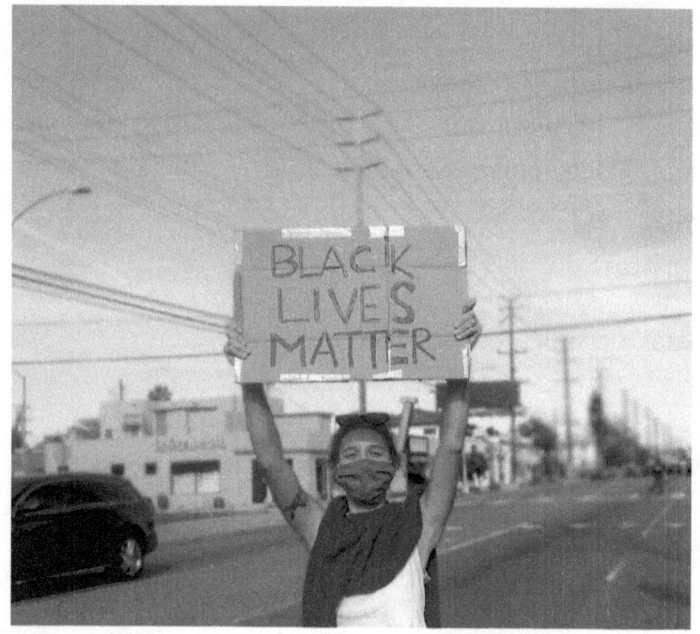

Name: Doug Eisenstark
Discipline: photography
Country: United States of America

2020:
One of the things I realized about lockdown was that most of us weren't going to spend the time learning a new language or learn to flamingo dance or clean the house to really, really clean or get in shape. No, it seemed like the thing to do was to dig into the past and find comfort in the deepening of our own experience of what we knew best. I worried that I liked the lockdown too

much. I poked around the house and sent off rolls of undeveloped film from 30 plus years ago. Put new soundtracks on old movies. And got my photo archive together. And many of them were of past demonstrations I had taken in photos and film. Early 70's: anti-War in Washington DC and University of Kansas, the 80's: anti-nuclear rallies at Seabrook, Massachusetts and New York City. Then not much until 2016. Woman's March Pt. 2, Muslim Ban at LAX.

Probably photography is the art I do best and I see my photographs as Evidence that for 1/60th of a second this event photographed existed on this planet. I don't set up photos for a "shoot" - I think using lights is a cheat and would never ask anyone to pose for me or otherwise stage a photo. As a kid I used to like to cut out pictures from National Geographic and just keep them around. Their photos were always so striking and you could tell right away they were National Geographic photos. But now it seems that striking, iconic, heroic picture has become the only photo worth taking. They look staged although I'm sure the animal ones aren't but now they just look so darn perfect. And everyone was to put these dramatic photos up on InstaGram. I bring this up because I'm a "street photographer", a "Decisive Moment" photographer. It's a Zen thing. Yeah, I know it sounds pretentious.

I also have to say I have an internal prohibition on taking pictures of word text. It seems cheap to have a message displayed "literally" in what should be a non-verbal medium.

By mid-April, the lockdown seemed like forever (what did we know?). Habits changed, shopping on-line for masks, buying food for a week, hoping to find a good five season streaming series. (A two hour movie wouldn't make a dent in all the time we had at home.) It rained in April, always an event in Los Angeles. And then for me I had my- "the sh-t got real" moment. Driving home from Smart and Final with my groceries I see a man sitting on a little wall and an ambulance parked near. I parked at a distance and watched in the car through the light rain. He was in his thirties, robust and otherwise healthy looking and holding a grocery bag. But it seems he can't breathe. He can barely stand up. The ambulance crew is talking to him for twenty minutes from a distance. And I had my camera. I guess another (a real?) photographer would have gone over and taken pictures. But I sat in the car for half an hour and took a few shots over that time. I didn't mean to upset him any more nor embarrass him in any way. Already neighbors were watching from their yards. Finally he was put on a gurney and taken into the ambulance. I lifted my camera and put my eye to the viewfinder and snapped. At that moment the ill man seemed to look straight at me and into the camera. I was mortified. Had he seen me taking a photo of him or was he only looking at the car or just generally in my direction? I take the camera home and put the file on the computer. I zoom in, more and more. Its inconclusive when blown up, more pixels than image. I tell myself that its a document, that someone has to show the events of this year even if its such a small gesture.

Artist, ART, & Story: A Moment in Time, 2020: International

Then in May the demonstrations started. I had wanted to join but I never knew where or when the demonstrations were. I am older now and at risk for Covid so I didn't want to rush in lightly. Of course, I have long been appalled by injustice to the Black community. My friends who turn on their heels when they see a cop. In 2019, my male Black students, shortly after a rash of police shootings, began wearing suits and ties and eschewing their normal street clothes. I never asked or commented about it but I prayed for their protection. But for myself I felt neither lucky nor "blessed" (which seems horrific a term under the circumstances) but acknowledging having aware of my (male) white privilege not to have confront such injustice personally. (And this extended to Covid- my zoom and online business sustaining me without being "essential". So few coworkers or friends got seriously ill.)

Then in May, there was the murder of George Floyd and Black Lives Matter. I watched the TV of the crowds in Santa Monica 3 miles away while simultaneously hearing the sound of police sirens rushing down Lincoln Blvd. But that day of all days I had work at home and could not to go out. The next weeks in my apartment I would hear other sounds of BLM marchers. Down Lincoln? From Abbott Kinney? Venice Beach? I would look on the internet and only see pictures of what had happened earlier.

Then one day I was walking around my neighborhood taking pictures on Lincoln and a smaller group of marchers were walking by and I followed. And I was glad to join in the march and most all of them were wearing masks. I didn't really like to take photos of marchers. How would they be used? What if the cops got them to identify people? I took pictures of the cops hanging around and joined the march. The marchers were half if not a third my age. They walked really fast and after a few blocks instead of being in front of the march I was at the back. Most of the marchers were soon disappearing. But one woman at the back saw my camera and me taking pictures.

I imagine that under her mask she smiled. In any case, on that day she raised her cardboard sign with the slogan on it above her head. I took the picture. It was a nice afternoon, around 6 PM, a great time for photography. I think its a striking photograph and while perhaps not worthy of National Geographic, for a 60th of a second, marchers, she and I and a sign with a message on it existed on Lincoln Boulevard.

Website: http://taiqi.me

Hadiya Finley

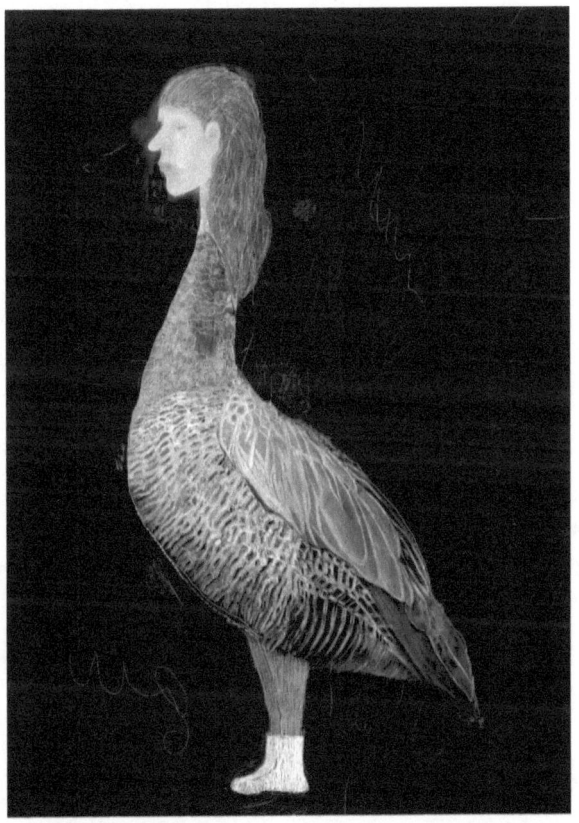

Name: Hadiya Finley
Discipline: Sculpture/drawing
Country: United States of America

2020:
I woke up on the morning of Chinese New Year's Day to the sound of the lion dancers in the street below my 14th floor Guangzhou apartment. Somehow the sound was hollow and when it died away it faded into dead silence.

That moment I can not forget, as the start of the coronavirus pandemic. We had met the evening before for New Year's Eve dinner as usual, but my daughter-in-law, Nora's, father, the top respiratory doctor in the country, having just returned from Wuhan, did not have good news. This was a new disease that spread by person to person contact and was extremely contagious. Everything would be cancelled. Wuhan was to be locked down and we watched the news reports of the growing number of cases, keeping an anxious eye on the case numbers in Guangzhou, which remained thankfully low. A day or so later, as restaurants were still open we met family in a local duck restaurant where we ate in a private room. We learned that one of Nora's cousins, who had been at dinner New Year's Eve had a fever and was at a fever clinic awaiting results of a Coronavirus test. We had an anxious night waiting for news which turned out to be good and would not mean we'd all have to be quarantined. When we left the private room we were dining in, those few diners in the main room applauded Nora's dad when they recognized him. He had become a well known figure in Guangzhou for his work on SARS in 2003, now he is a national hero. These first days of the pandemic will stay in my memory, cemented by the anxious feeling that invaded me, the odd quiet of the city streets, the new protocol of the apartment complex guards with face shields and temperature guns. Only residents allowed to enter, even deliveries had to be left outside the gate. We checked an app on our phones to see where new cases had been identified. One family in my compound had been identified and all residents received notices under their doors. This explained the guards wearing face shields and plastic bags.

At some point it was decided necessary to extract the maid from her home village where she had gone for Chinese New Year Celebrations and bring her back to work. We were all in the house and needed to be fed. A driver was hired to fetch her, though it was understood that the village had been barricaded and she would have to make a plan to meet him.

School began for my grandkids, 9 and 13, virtually. I was able to help quite a bit with my fourth grade granddaughter, helping her especially with English and Social studies projects. My daughter-in-law took it extremely seriously learning 7th grade math herself in order to work with 7th grade son. I got a thrill when I was able to get the science project circuitry to use a potato to light up a bulb. We also participated in a dramatization of a United Nations refugee crisis. The virtual learning routine was taken seriously throughout the whole lockdown period.

In all this time in the apartment of my son's family I did very little of what is familiar to me. At times I missed being creative and attempted projects that I could do in a space where I was a guest. Myself, usually messy finding this restraint difficult. I had a spate of reading, a try at resurrecting a partial clay figure, some iPad drawing, perusing digital magazines, wrote an article for the expat women's magazine, tried unsuccessfully to do Sculpy dolls, and plenty of Facebook. I mostly made friends with my IPad. My flight home in May was cancelled, my visa was extended and then cancelled. I was later able to get a new resident permit.

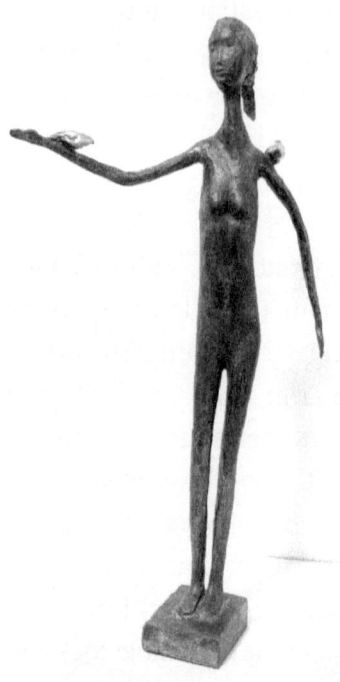

When news that the virus was now affecting people in the US and I had conversations with family and friends at home and realized how it was not being treated in any way as seriously as people did here, I became anxious and upset. The same anxiety that had gripped me at the beginning returned as I thought of the people I cared about now dealing with it and wondering when it would be safe to go home.

Here in China, things eased, people had begun going back to work, they opened Wuhan and waited to see if there would be new cases. There were, but this passed. People returning from abroad also brought new cases, triggering new regulations and eventually blocking entry to foreigners. People here were getting back to normal, though we debated such things as the safety of restaurant dining. Showing restraint paid off as people who had eaten in certain restaurants found themselves quarantined when cases were discovered. Restaurants were closed for weeks. You could always get take out though. Eventually the kids went back to school, wearing masks and observing dozens of new regulations. Homeschooling ended. I could spend my mornings at my own apartment and completed the projects abandoned when the pandemic hit. Just a year later now I have been to the foundry to see about finishing those pieces I brought in before Christmas.

Life here is cautiously back to normal, with some differences. Everyone wears a mask in public, they still check temperatures when entering many places. There are not as many foreigners and our Expat women's group is meeting, as people slowly come back to China, but with fewer clubs and activities. So I am still spending much time on my son's couch with my IPad. I am trying to get motivated to do things...

Website: http://www.barefootbird.com

Our Ever Changing World: Through the Eyes of Artists: Book 14

Lisa Maureen Campognone

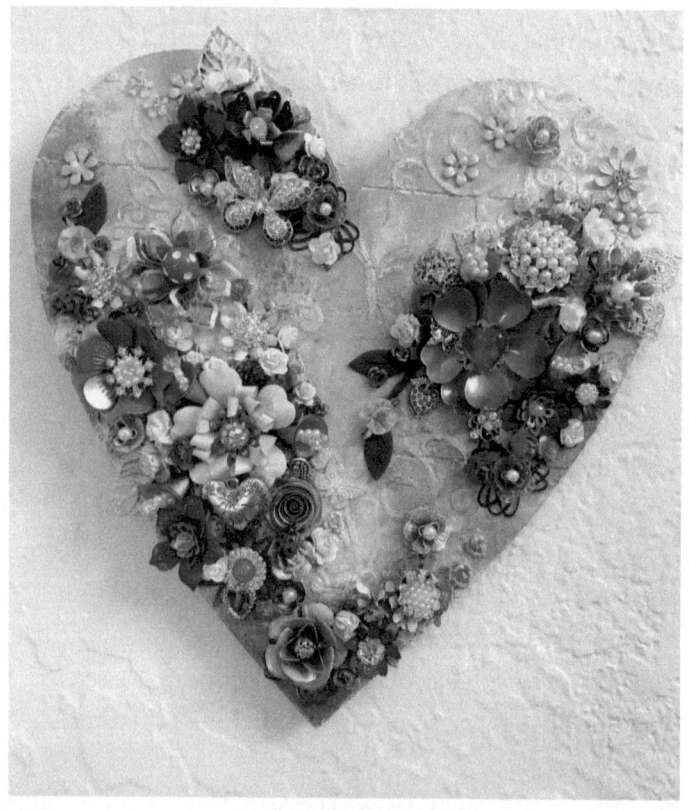

Name: Lisa Maureen Campognone
Discipline: Costume Design
Country: United States of America

2020:
I have always been considered 'sensitive' by family members. The truth of the matter is that I am an empath and I have been this way my entire life. It has made it very difficult at times to be social, as I pick up on everyone's

energy and emotions around me. Being in a group setting can become so overwhelming there are times I want to say goodbye as quickly as I have said hello.

During quarantine the energy of our world was completely different than I've ever felt in my 52 years. The fear was overwhelming and the sadness was deeply rooted into our earth.

I wanted to help somehow, I needed to give people reassurance and hope. Our world needed love and the support of angels. While I am not religious, just spiritual, Angels represent miracles and our world was in great need.

I started creating angel wing pins, angel wing ornaments, wall hangings and then an extra large angel. I wanted to share my love, appreciation and support, especially to those in the medical community, first responders anyone putting their lives at risk every day. They were angels in my opinion.

Our world needed healing energy, support, encouragement and togetherness. My creations are filled with flowers and generally bring a sense of happiness to others. I started creating videos of my creations with encouraging statements. I joined as many social media outlets as I could and began posting daily, trying to send encouragement and support to others.

My Angels, like all my creations, are filled with an eclectic mix of vintage and new jewelry components. I embellish my handmade metal flowers with shoe buckles, bridal jewelry components, chandelier components, fabrics-lace, velvet, silk, feathers, beads, any jeweled embellished buttons, snaps, hooks, jeweled spacers and links, decorative wire, handmade mulberry paper flowers, glass beads, rhinestones, pearls, crystals, lamp work beads, charms, brooches, earrings, filigree, acrylic flowers, cabochons, buttons...all things shiny or with a glitter.

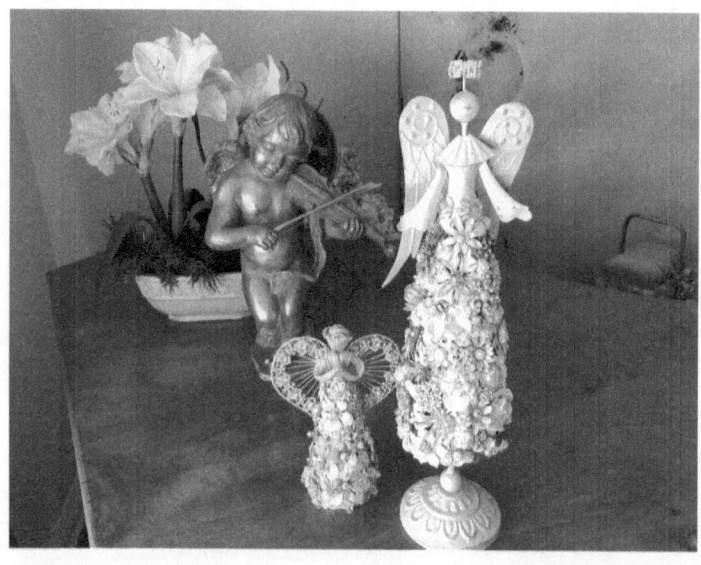

My treasures have a general theme of Love ♥ Peace, acceptance, hope, family, happiness, togetherness of all. I pray our world can come together.

Website: http://www.lisamaureen.com

Dixie O'Connor

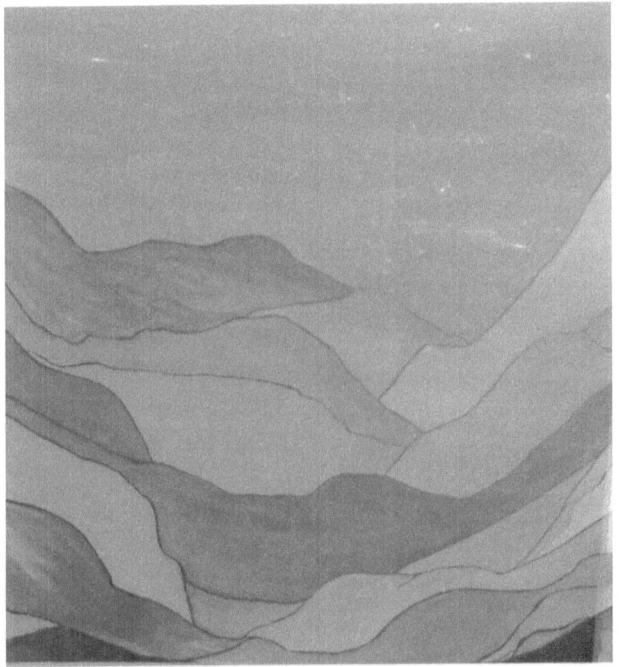

Name: Dixie O'Connor
Discipline: Painting and Ceramics
Country: United States of America

2020:
2020: The year that never seemed to end!
Many events and realizations in 2020 impacted my life and my ability to create art! Early on, there were hints of a virus in China. Few in the USA were concerned because it wasn't in THIS country—a country protected by God! Few seemed to realized how rapidly it would travel across the globe—that it would become a pandemic which,

would disrupt lives as nothing before. With no response plan and a president who refused Pfizer's offer of the vaccine (so they sold it to other countries!), there were over 300,000 deaths by December 31, 2020! Harrowing stories continue of death and long-term/life-long suffering from COVID-19. I know some of these people! The purported hoax has not only taken lives, it has stripped the livelihood of millions more. Families have been thrown into debt by the catastrophic cost of care and treatment! We have experienced our hopes and the hopes of America derailed—the America that has always been there to respond to and rescue other countries, other peoples. With neither government action, nor rescue of the USA by allies now estranged, our economy declined and we became the laughing stock of the world.

As 2020 unfolded, and in the wake of escalating police violence (for instance, George Floyd and Breonna Taylor), I, a woman born in The South, have realized we are all racist. This is learned, carried over for the past 400 or so years. Slavery was supposedly abolished a couple of hundred years ago, but has been preserved in our DNA, in our social and business lives. Our language and behaviors are fraught with racist remarks, words, actions. I am appalled at the treatment of people of color (Native peoples and all black/brown/darker skinned people) by privileged, elitist whites many of which promulgate it and justify their actions through symbols of oppression such as 6MWE (6 Million Jews Were Not Enough) in demonstrations across the nation! The overt act of making others who look different or share another religion or philosophy "less than" has become an accepted behavior. I was forced to acknowledge that despite two wars against slavery and fascism (in which members of my family fought) the USA, incited via The White House, was fast moving towards becoming a fascist government.

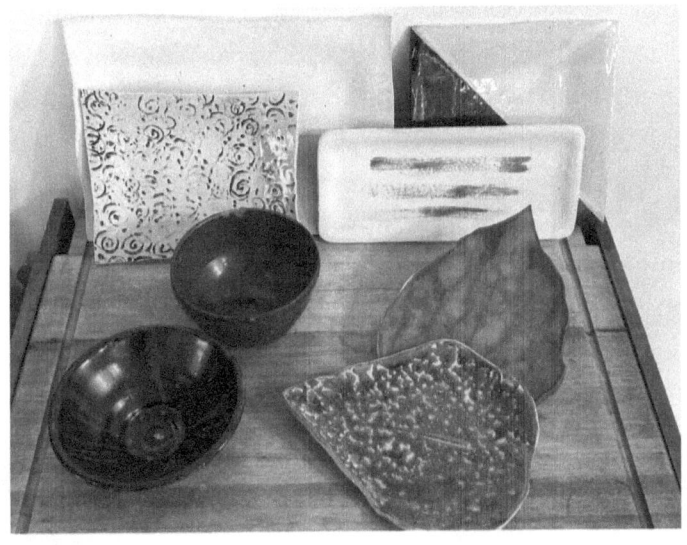

In the first quarter, I painted very little. I could not paint beautiful art in such dark, ugly times. But I could throw pottery! Throwing clay was physical, grounding, centering. Center the clay; allow myself to become centered; leave the ugliness behind. Creativity abounded. I went to the studio 3-4 days a week. I made platters and bowls; some thrown, others hand-built. Then, suddenly, I received email notification that the studio was closed until further notice! All tools and unfinished pieces sat on my shelf at the studio for six months before I was allowed make an appointment to retrieve them, glaze anything that had been bisque fired, bring home finished pieces. My creative life had been effectively dismantled.

My spirit plummeted. Yet, as a "Blue Dot" in a "Red" state, there was a spark that allowed me to hope Biden/Harris would somehow make history and begin to change America's trajectory. I wanted to be a part of the solution, so acquired and placed campaign signs. With November's Presidential Election results, though hotly contested by the outgoing administration, my faith in the American people is beginning to be restored. It seems fitting that 100 years after passing the Nineteenth Amendment, this country at last has a woman Vice President!

Alexander Graham Bell said, "When one door closes, another door opens." I look forward to the opening of the next door, the next chapter. I have begun to allow myself to dream and to enjoy the process of living and creating. And I am painting once again!

Website: http://dixieoconnor.com

William Hemmerdinger

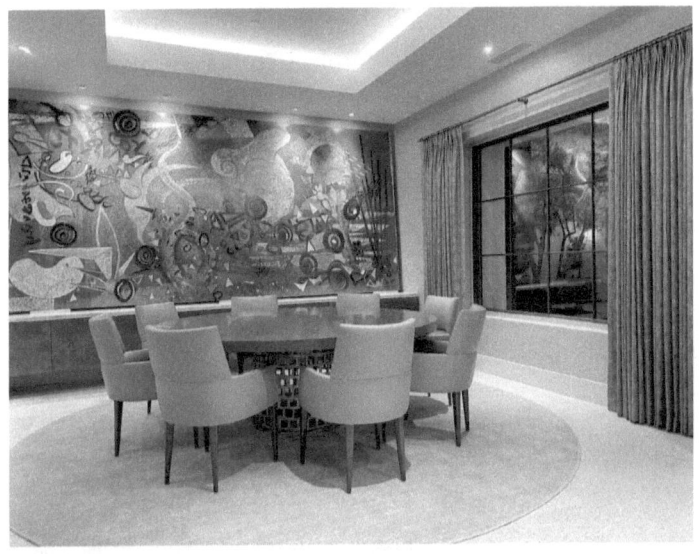

Name: William Hemmerdinger
Discipline: Painting
Country: United States of America

2020:
Bardez II, measures 7' x 15' and was painted during the pandemic year 2020. Acrylic on canvas.

Bardez II is the most recent of works created for my Lexicon Series.

This recent year, faced with an out-of-control pandemic, I stayed largely in my Massachusetts studio. Three thousand miles from Los Angeles, it is about as far away from home as I can be, nesting in the last of the cottages on a rural road, on the verge of the North Atlantic.

Much of my studio time in 2020, was devoted to the large painting shown here. In both title and subject matter, the painting entitled Bardez II, is about a place other than this wooded New England perch. The California desert depicted at night.

Fifty-five years ago, skipping out of Burbank High School classes, I followed a few like-minded rebels to the folk artist John Ehn's hodge-podge estate The Old Trapper's Lodge on San Fernando Road. From there, catching a few rides, I made my way into the desert.

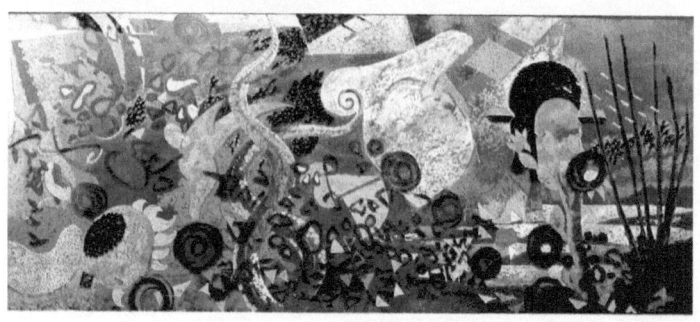

Evenings meant bright conversation, spiraling eddies of smoke and dust, plus laughter rising up among to date palms, creosote bushes, larrea, brittlebush, chuperosa, sage, cone pine, cholla, opuntia, barrel cactus. A solemn quiet came later.

Website: http://www.williamhemmerdinger.com

Linda Saccoccio

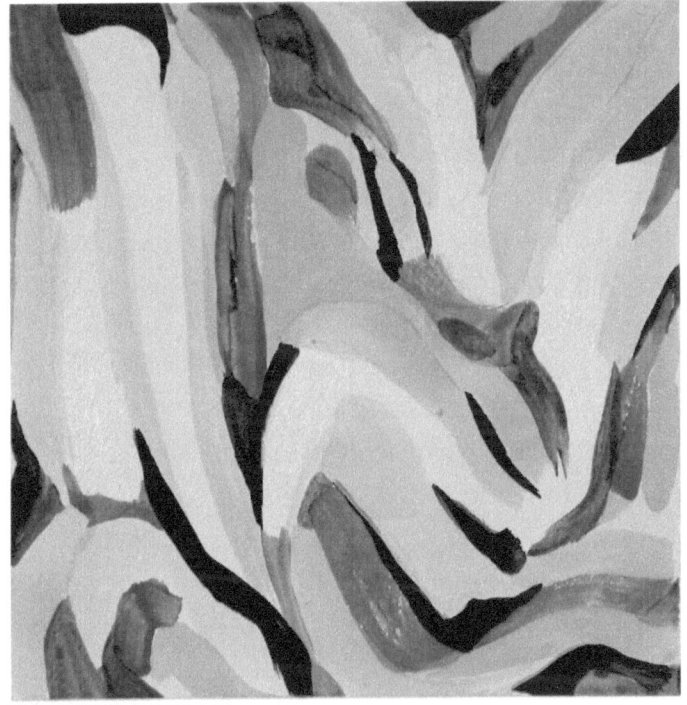

Name: Linda Saccoccio
Discipline: Fine Artist
Country: Unites States of America

2020:
Focus Year: 2020 — A Stone in My Shoe No More

At the start of 2020, my 91-year-old father was "not doing well." This I learned from my mother. Our phone conversations over the last three years usually precipitated long flights from my home in California to Rhode Island. For three years, my father's health vacillated, and the process was taking a toll on my mother, his sole caregiver. I knew that I was needed but after two surgeries for cancer—in 2017 and 2019—I was preparing for a third. Between January and February, I resolved to switch doctors. By the end of March, I had a case of Shingles, a symptom of stress. At that time, we learned we were in a global pandemic. Not knowing the severity of the corona virus, not wanting to know the illness firsthand, I followed orders to self-isolate.

I moved my studio to my home, and in all honesty, it was a welcomed move. I needed to focus in a new way. I needed change. I welcomed not rushing around to events of all kinds and feeling obliged to do things that were sometimes fulfilling, but at the same time drained or scattered my energy. As an introvert who had to work to be more social, because it must be "good" for me, I needed a break. I needed to be patient, to witness my daily surroundings. I moved here from New York City in 2003, expecting a change of pace, but I had yet to take advantage of the opportunity.

The richness that I was able to access from my home was profound. I began to taste hints of the life of a monk, which I had often craved. I gave priority to yoga, meditation, spiritual teachings, and also to poetry readings and art talks offered globally online. Gurumayi Chidvilasananda, head of the Siddha Yoga lineage, began to offer live satsangs to help support the global community during this unprecedented, challenging time. She reminded us that we have the tools to face the extremes at hand. Discipline, to make my art, write poetry, and do spiritual practices held my focus, and I felt liberated. Limitations delivered the simple life that I desired for too long.

Working at home, oil paints were not an option, but that was okay, since bladder cancer obliged me to figure out how to work without solvents and other toxic mediums. I had not yet resolved this issue but painting in oils at home in the communal space was out of the question. Fortunately, for some years when I wasn't painting in oils, I made small paintings with water-based paints in books of handmade paper from Nepal and India. This medium offered spontaneity and delight in its immediacy. I developed a rapport with the medium, and a knack for allowing the paints fluidity and color to carry and deliver a composition that was resonant.

These paintings in gouache and watercolor were quickly taking on new life and evolving. Perhaps I was influenced by the views of ocean and skies. The openness from working on slightly larger paper also had impact, as did a shift in mindset. The slower pace of being at home, not getting in the car, allowed for an intimacy to evolve and influence my personal agency and my relationship with painting. It felt like I was restoring my original passion for painting. I recognized the pleasure from childhood that had been a constant companion to return to if I strayed. While working, I began to make contact with intangible energy more directly, more assuredly. Holding a meditative open mind, I developed trust in my silent guide. As inspiration for these works on paper, I would often read passages of poetry, until I was moved enough to let their imagery and feeling spawn a painting or colored pencil drawing. Drawing is a process that is deeply core to me. Now I have added the pleasure of using colored pencils to meander on the toned page.

The year cautiously unfolded. Navigating the phases of a pandemic, seeing the videos of people in Italy on their balconies singing or playing music, was a sweet yet melancholy whisper of both the potency of humanity and life's fragility. Who would this virus touch, and would it render them alone in death? There were many horrors, as the humor and creative expressions carried us along.

In May, I had my third surgery for low-grade bladder cancer with my new surgeon/urologist, followed by six installments of chemotherapy over a seven-week period. My father continued to weaken, and my sister Dona and her son Richard stepped in to help my parents. Dona and Richard shared regular updates, anecdotes and photos. Their technological advantage enabled me to FaceTime with my father. It wasn't safe for me to travel, as I had every other time he neared death, but I could see and talk to him more than I ever had before. He was becoming more direct, simpler, curious and sensitive. I saw a side of him I rarely saw before. Our weekly visits were sacred moments of honoring his life, which he was navigating with grace and an even pace, which his monk-like side offered him.

He turned 92 on the 29th of June, a palindrome of numbers. It was amazing to see him make it. He lived into August, but one Friday night he fell, gashing his head on a door edge. It seemed he sensed his demise. A man who never cried released tears as Dona and my mother tended him on the bloody bathroom floor.

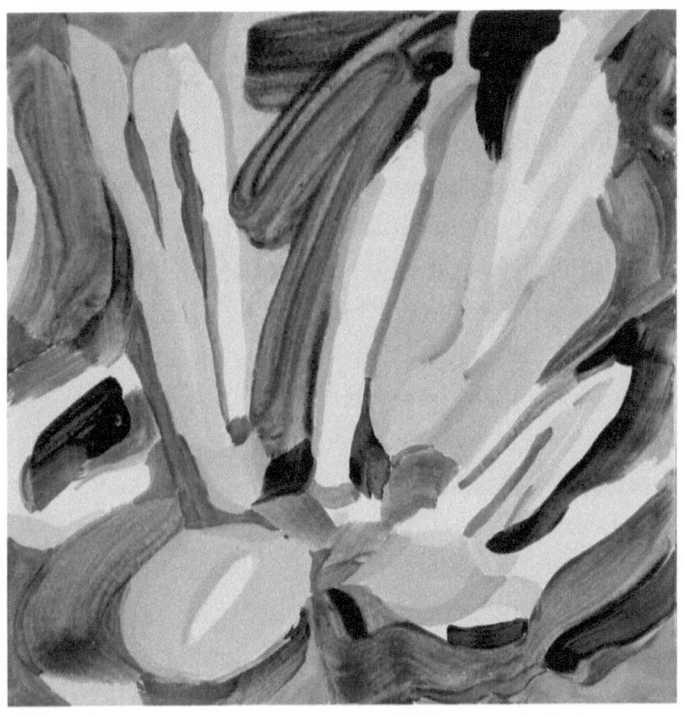

The next day he was bed-ridden. It was the 15th of August, the Assumption of Mary, a favorite day of my Nonni, Celia, who said the water was blessed that day. It was the birthday of three of his grandchildren, including Richard and Vani Alana, my first daughter. My Nonni, who died in the 1970's, came to me in a dream, and

I sensed her beckoning my father. The next morning, Sunday the 16th of August, 2020, my father Peter Saccoccio died. He left his 88-year-old wife, my mother Esther, a widow. Although sad and mysterious, his ending felt justly timed. He gave all he had, all he could, and he left with one last breath in Dona's company.

Inconceivably, I had to honor his life from a distance. Never could I have predicted a pandemic would keep me from his death and the rituals to follow, but here I was, extending what I could to make contact with this new reality. When one doesn't see family on a regular basis, the belief in finality, to never see them alive again, is vague at best. I sensed his presence in animals: a hawk, a green bug, a baby lizard, small birds in flight with the leaves blowing in the cradle of a hot springs destination. His energy was palpable. He was free to visit me without the limitations of a body. He could offer his goodbyes and blessings for my life and work, in a way he never could when he was alive.

To say my relationship with my father was complicated is an understatement. Although he felt love and concern, he was outspoken and rejected harshly my life work as a painter. It took his close brushes with death to soften and open him to ask about my work with earnest intent. Toward the end, I sensed him releasing the conditions that caused him to lash out at me. In turn I felt and continue to feel released from his limitations, able to live unapologetically the life of artist and poet.

Artist, ART, & Story: A Moment in Time, 2020: International

In September, I couldn't host my 60th birthday party with friends, so I booked a cabin in Big Sur, a place that has inspired me before. Then the fires raged for weeks in the area. I cancelled my Big Sur cabin, and booked another one in Paso Robles. The temperatures soared to 106°, then subsided with steady conditions of ash and smoke. Still the little cabin by a dry creek-bed and a field of wild animals was a respite for healing from chemotherapy and the loss of my father. He even visited me in a dream there, the day before my birthday. In the dream he offered apologies and acceptance, acknowledgement of my artistic work. In Paso Robles, my husband and I visited Bruce Munro's spectacular installation, "Field of Lights" at Sensorio. It was a gift, a visual infusion and creative incentive as I began my 60th year.

When we returned to Santa Barbara, smoke filled the air. We stayed indoors with the Omega Institute hosting an online retreat with Pema Chödrön, the Buddhist nun and student of the late Chogyam Trungpa. It reaffirmed my practice of consistent daily meditation, which in turn, supports my creative work.

Feeling restored after months of working at home, I was drawn back to the studio. During the fall I spent days reclaiming my space in preparation for new work. I was able to sort through and discard things I had accumulated and previously imagined I might need or use one day. I acknowledged the mediums that naturally attract me now, instead of those of days past. Editing out clutter gave the studio a fresh, welcoming appeal—clean, renewed, with order and calm. I established a routine that continues to develop. I am motivated to discover the possibilities in gouache and pencil. I foresee returning to oil paints with newly acquired sensibilities. I look forward to continued exploration of what is ready to develop with an altered perspective.

The cumulative loss of friends and family in 2020 humbled and shook me. It forced me to reorient myself in life and art, and to accept that I have been granted the time to develop my work further. I can follow the momentum of my life with creative enthusiasm, in part as homage to the losses of the year.

Website: https://www.lindasaccoccio.com

Remembering::

Paula A. Fiore, Wakefield, RI, November 24, 2020
Jackie Saccoccio, West Cornwall, CT, December 4, 2020
Kathy I. King, Santa Barbara, CA, December 16, 2020
My father, Peter Saccoccio, Johnston, RI, August 16, 2020
Stepmother-in-law, Karen E. Winick, West Hartford, CT, September 26, 2020

Maria Laura Hendrix

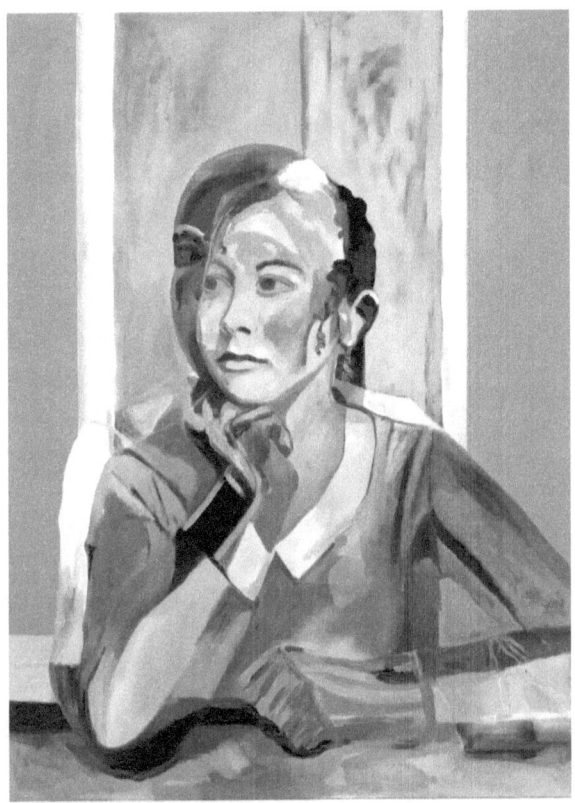

Name: Maria Laura Hendrix
Discipline: Painting
Country: United States of America

2020:
On a chilly morning in March of 2020, I got in my car and drove 1600 hundred miles round trip to pick up my daughter at her college dorm. On that morning the world was standing still in some ways as I drove down a freeway

across the country, with miles and miles of empty road in front of me. The governor of California had declared the order to shelter in place a few days prior. The news of COVID 19 pandemic was now real after months of speculation that it would not reach the United States. I was alone driving during rush hour on a road that is the lifeline of interstate traffic. The order from the governor of California to shelter in place was being observed as evidenced by the empty freeways. I drove south on the 101 and made my way east towards the I-40 at a steady seventy-five miles per hour. Something I had never before experience in L.A. traffic. The eerie feeling of the empty road held my attention through the entire trip. I drove past Barstow and crossed the California Nevada border with only the occasional semi truck in sight. The lonely road gave me comfort, with no cars in sight my attention was focused on the scenery with the signs of spring visible on the low laying shrubs. The dessert colors calming my senses as I tried not to think of the pandemic. With no radio and music I was left with only my thoughts as I counted the hours I had been on the road.

Something that has become apparent to me during this past year is my tendency to withdrawal inward, as a coping mechanism, when trying to make sense of the world around me. The idea of sheltering in place took on a psychological significance, for me. In some way I was going against the lockdown order but in another way that order hurled me into a deep state of self preservation. During that drive I took notice of the land like never before.

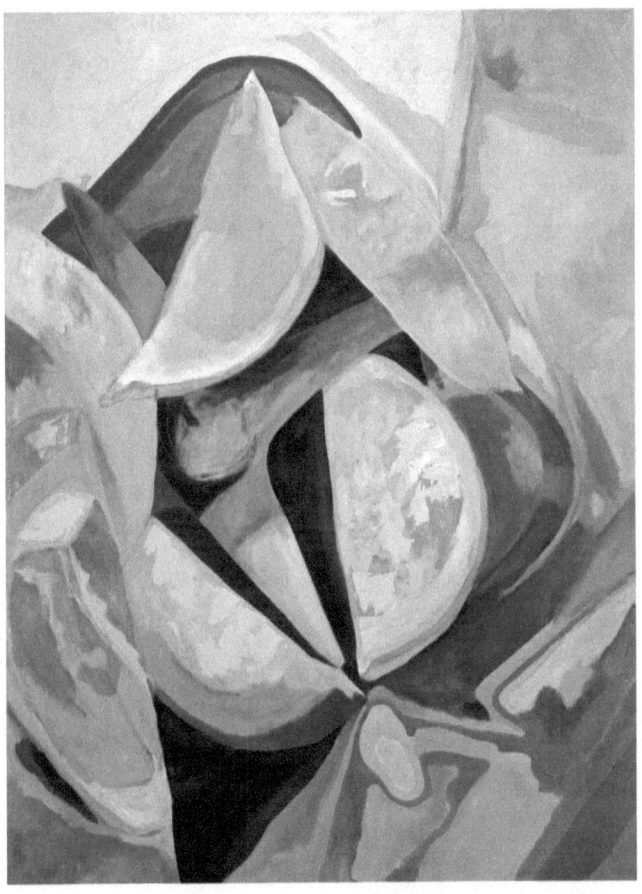

Pragmatically, I made my way down the I-40 and continued to countdown the hours left to travel. The vast vistas took my breath away as I drove up the mountain towards Flagstaff. The scenery changed into a forested land as the road meandered up the mountain side. Bordered by so many trees I felt enveloped by nature, it was a sight to remember. Alone yet surrounded by nature I continued driving towards my destination. As I entered New Mexico I saw for the first time the landscape that proves its name sake as the land of enchantment. I was enchanted by the vastness of the land with far away plateaus. The red orange sunset reflected on my rear view mirror reminding me of the time that had already passed. My thoughts began to wonder what the news were reporting? Anxiously I turned on the radio but all I heard was static. I therefore preoccupied myself seeing the miles traveled increase, signaling that I was getting closer to my destination. A pandemic was taking root through the land and my sole thought was in reaching my destination to make sure my daughter was safe. After twelve hours on the road I reached my destination and rushed to embraced my daughter. We drove with the news that New Mexico was no following suit and ordering its population to shelter in place. The scenery on the way back home was but a blur in my mind, we drove home with little clue of the events that would unfold later that spring and summer. Events that made little sense but that have shaken our country to the core. These events though surreal in some sense have presented the reality of many. That spring the news outlets were optimistic that we would return to normal as soon as a few months. That didn't happen.

Website: http://www.marialaurahendrix.com

Genie Davis

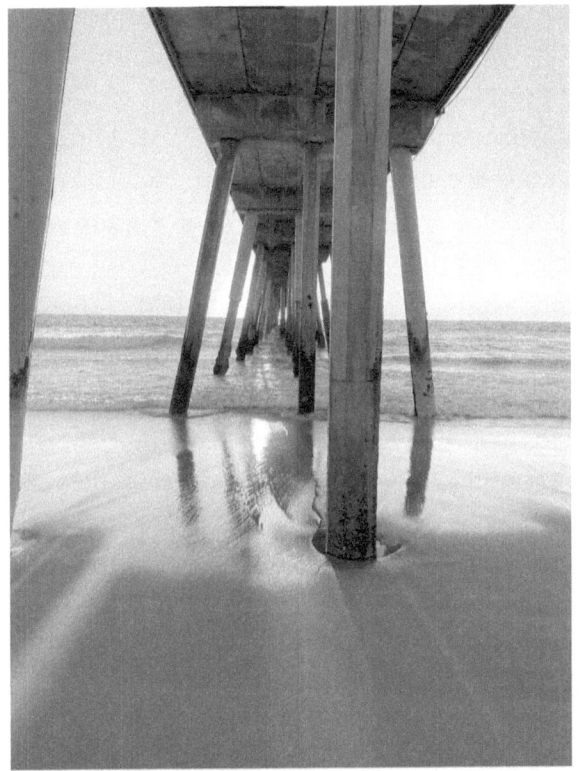

Name: Genie Davis
Discipline: writer
Country: United States of America

2020:
If I Had Known…

20/20 hindsight. 20/20 vision. Change comes in cycles and I suppose I was overdue; mostly I was on cruise control, thinking I was in control.

The year of our Lord 2020, the great pandemic, began auspiciously enough, as I ignored any news from China because "it can't happen here." My boyfriend and I were in a favorite deserted little desert town, Ajo, Arizona, which is trying to become an arts community. It has a wonderful arts-oriented complex of apartments created from a former high school; the attached elementary school is now an inn and conference center. I discovered it 5 years earlier and we made a visit then; this return was to be a peaceful start to what looked like a hectic year. If I had known…well, I would've asked to go to Vegas or NYC or Portugal. But there we were, enjoying veggie tamales and champagne and listening to coyotes' howl. We visited petroglyphs and took long walks in the desert and explored the town's old cemetery. On New Year's Day, after a mocha from the town's new and only coffee house, for the very first time ever I said "rabbit, rabbit, rabbit" which I heard was good luck. We even found a little artwork of a rabbit in the arts complex and posed for a selfie by it.

Back in LA, there were art openings, new restaurants to try, a press-comp-arranged birthday trip for my sweetie to a wild horse sanctuary and a luxury spa, plans to spend my birthday in New Orleans. But then hmmm, maybe we better not fly, how about driving to the Grand Canyon? Then hmm, maybe we don't want to be around that many people, maybe we should go to Big Sur? And finally, hmm, you might be contagious, let's just both stay home.

So, yes, the pandemic. And at first, my friends and my boyfriend and I were all afraid to be around each other, and just Zoomed, a word I had not even heard of until March. In person, I saw two people: my son whom I live with, and my 5-year-old grandson every weekend (plus daily chats with on Zoom to help out my daughter who is also immuno-compromised and so at high risk.) Magazines folded and slowed, some clients up and quit. But I zigzagged into a new and steady form of income with a book editing and ghostwriting company. Gradually, we all started taking walks and visiting in gardens and on patios, and going to the beach, always in our masks. If I had known, I would've wasted less time worrying about everything late at night. Things seemed to – normalize?

My 16-year-old kitty, a dear, friendly, loving little boy who our younger tortie girl cat adored, was doing great even though we knew he had kidney issues. His levels in March were almost back to normal thanks to a special diet and weekly sub-Q. The vet agreed with us that he had a few more good years ahead. But then, abruptly, he faltered in late June; in mid-July, he passed away. If I had known… I would've spent more time cuddling him on my bed where he often napped, and never complained once when he laid on top of my computer keyboard and deleted a file.

Our poor tortie girl was so miserable and sad that after three weeks we fostered a cat from a rescue intending to adopt, which was how that rescue operated. Unfortunately, that kitty was mysteriously ill and apparently had been separated from an older cat who had bonded with him, and turned out, per our vet, not to be 4 months old but 10 months old and underweight. When the illness couldn't be diagnosed, and that cat, too, was clearly in mourning, the rescue abruptly took the cat not to their vet for testing as we were told, but back to his soul mate at the rescue - and refused to return him. (Both remain there to this day, almost seven months later, still marked a months-earlier age.)

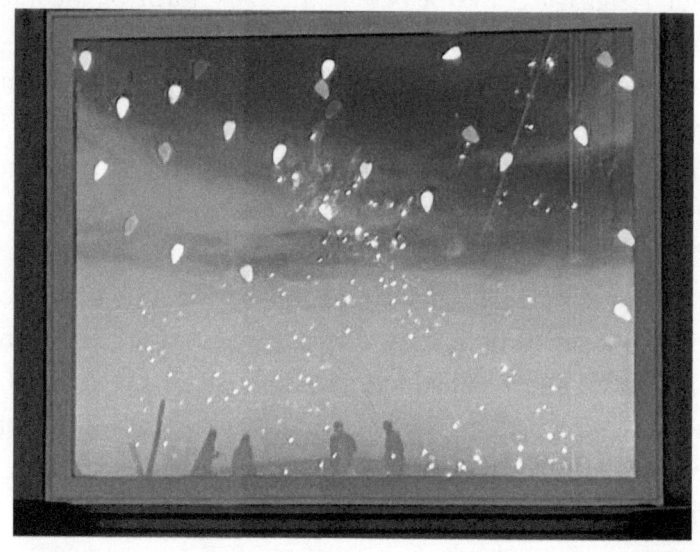

My ex-husband also passed away, and unlike our kitty, he was not mourned as beloved. My son and I breathed a collective sigh of relief that we'd no longer have to endure occasional e-mail pleas or diatribes. But, because nothing is simple, repeated contact with his girlfriend became a thing because for some reason I still haven't figured out, the coroner wouldn't turn the remains over to her, but wanted to give them to us, and complications ensued. If I had known…I would have changed my phone numbers and social media settings.

Then my daughter had relationship issues at home, that I futilely tried to stay out of. If I had known... trying not to be involved would lead to her decision to cut off all access to her own sweet little boy, on of all things, Grandparents Day, maybe I could've spread emotional flame retardant before her crash.

One friend lost her husband to a long-time disability; my dear cousin lost his business. My book editing gig went poof when a new owner cleaned house at the end of the year. If I had known...maybe I wouldn't have continually remarked on the good fortune of my friend's husband's apparently reasonable health, or the robustness of my cousin's business; maybe I would've made more space in my week to take on other side gigs instead of turning them down or putting them off.

Loss. That would be the theme of 2020. That and a certain myopic tendency of mine.

Except: I began to write poetry again. I made my formerly barren patio into an outdoor living space, including green fairy lights in fake trees and solar bulbs strung every which way from fence to townhouse, a real sofa and chairs, table and cushions, heat lamps and fresh paint. I learned to take photographs with intent and some artistry. I learned the pleasures of neighborhood and local beach walks; cooking – yes, oh-my-God-cooking from-scratch dishes; creating craft cocktails; sitting still and just talking; reading whole books again not just magazines; movies on, gasp, a television not in a theater. If I had known... any of these things would be delightful, much less all of them, maybe I would've started integrating them into my life sooner instead of feeling like my life was over. And, we got a new kitten, wholly ours, and totally adorable.

Gain. Not a theme but an ongoing practice. There are roads, not back, but on. There will always be a journey, a recognition, a transcendence that's indefinable but present, a look through the filaments of time into a new space.

It's not 20/20 hindsight, it's fuzzy foresight. It's not defensive or offensive actions, it's the ability to maneuver the slick spots, steep grades, sharp curves, rough road. It's not 20/20 vision, it's the donning of dark glasses to withstand the harsh glare of unwonted realities, it's the rose-colored shading of those dark glasses to see the undoubted pleasures still ahead. Yes, I'm getting myself a pair, and I hope you will, too. If I learned anything… 2021 doesn't come with any guarantees.

Website: http://www.diversionsla.com

Barbara Kerwin

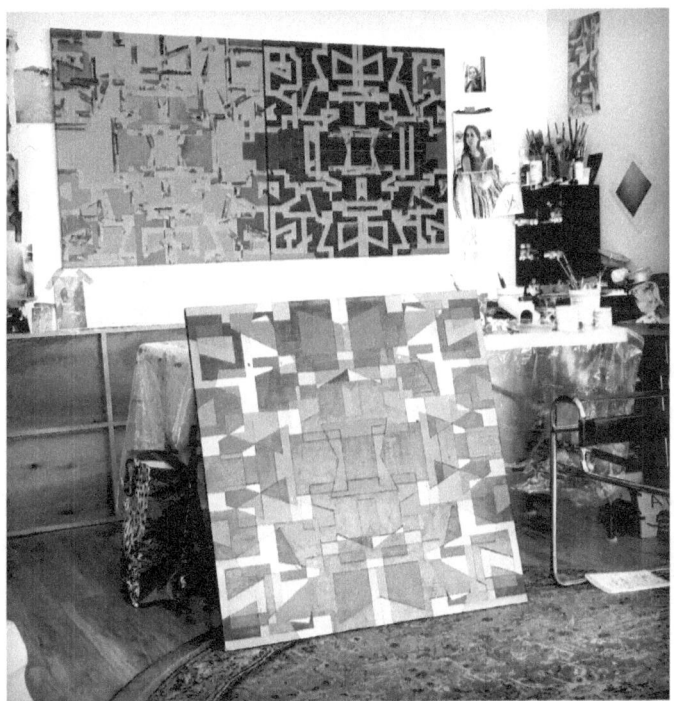

Name: Barbara Kerwin
Discipline: Painter
Country: United States of America

2020:

    Adventures in Los Angeles seize up March 9th. No more openings. Gatherings are not allowed. No networking is possible. A frightening virus has come to America and we are asked to isolate. I retire to "my stuff"—my painting studio, my writing pads and my library in my recently flood-remodeled home above the Rose Bowl. "Now" is about time. I have time. I have never had time—

I love time!! Life for me has been very demanding, and has required a lot from me. I have given to it my all, sometimes going a week without sleep just to keep up.

The canvases in my studio are complex puzzle paintings. None can be the same, yet they all have the same exact foundation, based on a diagram I drew on graph paper late into the night a while ago. I recognized it as "important"; a diagram of balance in complexity. This diagram has become the code from which all 7 large paintings are now constructed. each painting must be unique. It must become compelling enough to hold my attention—and it must tell the truth. Truth goes deep into the examination of a thing. With time I can see if it goes deep enough. If not, more paint. My painting is getting thick, even gooey. I use additives to accomplish this. I've been following my instinct to create this series. I don't have a venue. It doesn't matter.

I first made "Thoughts & Prayers", a response to gun violence in an ever angrier America. Lawmakers are adrift against each other and can't pass laws to do anything to stop it, so we send, instead, our thoughts and prayers. "Whistleblower" came next. It is a darkly mysterious piece in blacks and silvery bronzes with a faint gossamer light barely breaking through the fractured darkness. "Whistleblower" is about corruption being uncovered by decent people in a horrible time. I added more gels to help differentiate the dark surfaces and help to fracture that darkness. We observe how confusing partial glimpses may be. I'm now working on "Sheltering In", a complex, diptych of the same under-diagram, yet doubled, in a variety of reds. Unlike the previous two that varied the compositional emphasis, but did so symmetrically, in this painting I've mandated it to be painted without symmetry—so each step is an unknown, informed by the last. I have to study it and paint over with confidence until the color harmony does what is needed to come to finish. This diptych (36x72") is taking a long time.

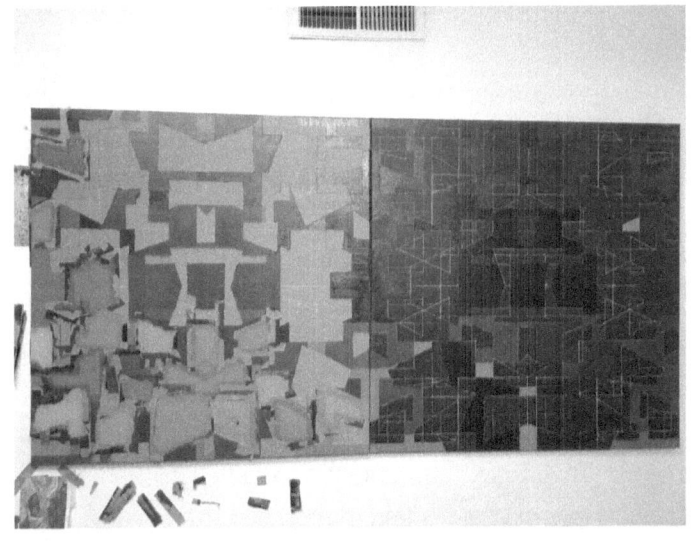

I deepened the golden hues in, "Patterns of Perception", by repainting its earlier too yellow iteration. It now happily hangs over my bed to awaken to, where I want to hug it— I look at it so much. The edges of the grid lines are so thick it deliciously begs to be touched. I'm also continuing a sub-set of abstract-shape portraits of people who are helping society. I've been finishing a Geo-Abstract portrait of "Rachel", my favorite newscaster. Her deep probes have gotten me through these difficult four years. Many riffs and divisions are now apparent between people—due to Trump's alternate realities. This has been distressing. No Fairness Doctrine in years. I've followed politics all my adult life, skipping classes to watch the Watergate Hearings. What happens at the top of government truly trickles down and becomes mimicked in the masses. If the president lies so do his followers. This concerns me. I have high ideals. A sense of hyper-vigilance and foreboding has alerted me throughout the term of this last presidency.

This has been my Covid-time: It has been a feeling time; an alert time. Grief experienced, has left me feeling naked and discombobulated. But grief, as much as I'd like to rush past it—takes time. In September, I turned my attention to writing letters for the upcoming election. I have to do what I can to help remove the blight at the top. Hurrah! In November, Joe Biden wins the presidency!!! Feelings of great joy!! Then, I join a Buddhist group to write letters to Georgia's voters, to help bring out more for their Senate run-off. This mass movement works!! The Senate goes blue!! But, on the same day the Senate winners are announced, the dark force in the White House has spewed a lie so big to his followers—his lie is that "he" won. He did not!! An insurrection on the Capitol while affirming the election was maneuvered by the incompetent loser and it shocks the world. Biden clearly won by more than seven million votes—it's not even close. Throughout this despicable action, gratefully the laws hold. Immediately the Congress returned that same night to confirm Joe Biden's win of the Presidency. Trump is the loser.

Artist, ART, & Story: A Moment in Time, 2020: International

This has been the most precarious of times, its not calm out there at all. 4000 people are dying each day of Covid. I have allowed myself this time to feel—it's always hard to feel so much, but I always have. Instead of rushing to accomplish tasks, I don't anymore. I do the tasks. But I resist that horrible chest-tightening feeling of rushing. Ugh! My big feelings are the reason I paint. As a child I learned I could make things and step outside of these big feelings and my body would coordinate nicely with me in doing so. It is pleasurable to look at the thing made when it completes. I strive to create balance in the world I occupy and my paintings reflect this. I understand why I paint many layers and go over things, especially if too rushed. I want the paintings I make to be dwelled with. If I can get to that, I know they are okay to go out into the world. Maybe their balance can help others as they help me? I spoke to Roland about my dogged preferences to make this type of painting—even though it's not the trend. He laughed, and said, "Exactly! Why else would you make paintings?" I laughed, too. Roland always encouraged me. He came to every show I made—until he couldn't any longer. Before his death he told me to quit my job and just paint—that the world needed me now. I am sad Roland left, I have a photo of him and his Dawn in my kitchen. During Covid-time I have framed pictures of everyone I have really loved, warts and all, and peppered my spaces with memories of them. They are the texture of me. I need to take time to honor what is loved, here or past. These paintings represent my simple task of living and loving. Even in a world this unsettled.

My life has been about figuring things out, thus, my puzzle paintings. They are hard and take time—they won't let me rush. Grief times are peculiar. I've tried to rush through it in the past, but no, it is a process, it's slow. There are also times that are so joyful it feels like Christmas!—and I never want those times to stop. None of these last. But we have remembrances. I've seen painful losses turn back into the richness of life. My aunt said, after a funeral long ago, that the hardest thing in life is to accept it. She seemed wise at the time, but I had no idea what she meant. I was young and filled with my dreams. The poet Rilke tells us about life that "being here is much, and because all this that's here, so fleeting, seems to require us and strangely concerns us." Like my aunty's saying, there is something profound in there. This, then, is the gift of Covid-time. It has cast its light on each of us, in just such a way. For me, I am surprised to find I don't mind being alone. I see I am gracious here. My whole self is occupied. I have hard stuff to figure out. My daughter Genni asks me to contemplate what it means to be vulnerable? I've decided it is a part of what it means to be human, and that is, after all, what interests me.

Website: http://www.barbarakerwin.com

Debbi Green

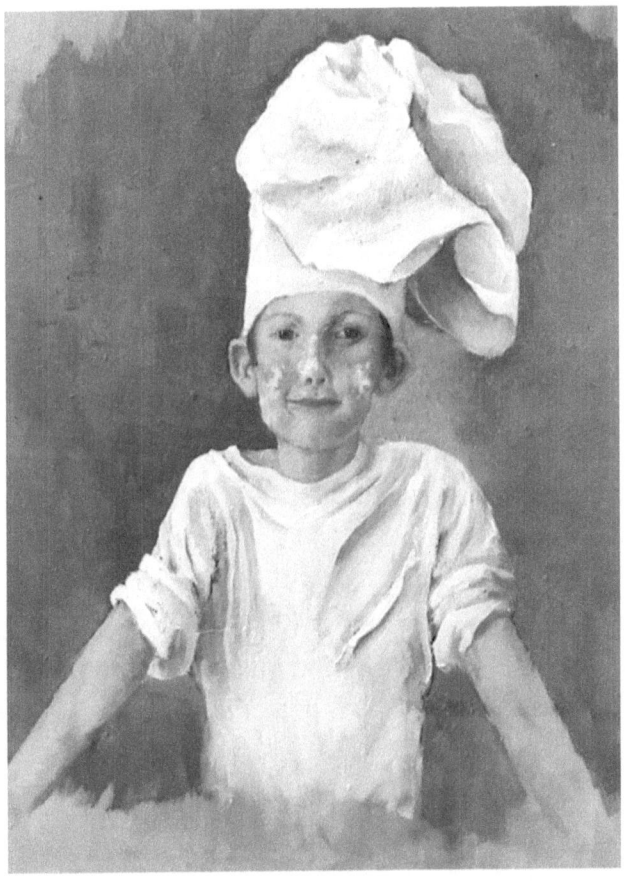

Name: Debbi Green
Discipline: painting
Country: United States of America

FIRST MONTH - MARCH
As I stood in my home studio, looking out onto the lake in Westlake, I thought to myself what dubious timing I have.

I had been subletting an art studio at Channel Islands Artist Studios. My expectations of a studio, an art community and being somewhat close to home would be an ideal place to tryout all the ideas swimming in my head. Although, after six months, I decided not to renew my lease. That was Feb. 28th, 2020.

Just prior to that, I did a favor for a dear friend. My friend had been catching feral cats in her neighborhood, so that she could have them neutered and then released. It was a very good plan that had been working for months. The last time at the veterinarians, the doctor said he would be happy to do just that, after this one gives birth!! That favor was taking home a brother and sister tabby 'team'. That was Feb. 17th, 2020.

One more item I added to my home, was my childhood piano that had been in storage, forever. I had arranged for the movers to come, a month later for the tuner and then in 3 weeks, start my piano lessons. The movers came Feb. 15th, 2020.

SIXTH MONTH – AUGUST
As I stand back and look at the 3 easels, with new artworks in progress, I am filled with gratitude. I am in a situation that has given me the time, with no pressure, to explore new mediums, subjects and be in the comfort of my own home.

I have a friend, who lives nearby so we are able to walk and talk every other day. Our conversations always start or end with the simple fact that we are safe, healthy, didn't lose a job (tho we are learning how to keep things/business going), and we have healthy loved ones.

We discuss our accomplishments and failures and discuss how we are coming along, in our separate ventures. It is so hard to explain to my 'right-brained' friend about art. But I try! I tell her that it is my meditation, AND problem solving. It is a dream, a game and sometimes a struggle. How challenging myself with each blank canvas, is what painting is about.

For example, I have started painting people. If you know me at all, I have painted farm animals most of my career. With the omission of people in my daily life, that I am normally surrounded by, now I'm bringing total strangers into my home? I find it so damn interesting and it just happened. It is a beginning.

I also starting using acrylics for some abstracts, just to explore and paint larger. Me! The one who paints within the lines. With details. And color, lots of color. These new works are all very neutral. Talk about being a reflection of me. My life as become a bit stark and I do not mean that in a negative way. I just do not need to say as much as I usually do.

I think these 'shifts' in my work comes from my journaling or 'morning pages'. Hand written pages, first thing in the morning ... from my heart, down my arm and onto the page. It is a way of emptying out some of the garbage that gets stuck in my brain or heart. I always thought that what I needed to do, as an artist, was to perfect what I have always done. You know that 'Master it' thing. That has been so limiting. But that is OK.

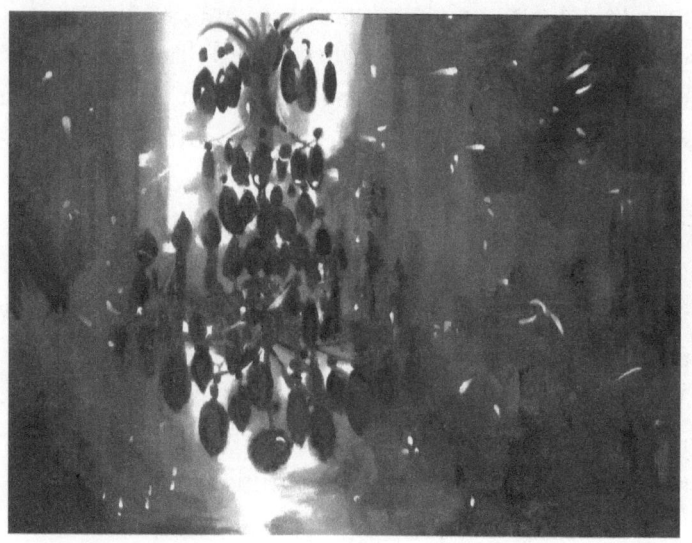

Having a need or want, to paint, is my passion. I am enthusiastic about it. It makes me smile. I do not need to explain it to artists, only for those damn "Bios". Does anyone really read those? Anyway, I love this gift of exploring.

I am also loving that Vinnie plays fetch with me. Only about 6 times a day but that makes him happy. No! I did not teach him that. And he is 16 pounds, all muscle! On the other hand, 7 pound Cookie has not learned to meow yet but makes the dreamiest 'chirp'. She likes to wash her mousey in her water bowl, a couple times a day. And

NO, I did not teach her that, either. What a gift to share my home with these two.

The piano tuner came and said that it was a fabulous 48 key upright. However I have not been able to find a teacher that wants to teach a beginner on Zoom. Bummer. I have remembered a few ditties from my past. You see, I was taught to play by ear, so I never learned to read music. There is a jazz player deep down inside and is just struggling to mimic or play along with Jamie Cullum or Herbie Hancock but these ears do not work the same as when I was a preteen. I will keep learning.

TENTH MONTH – DECEMBER
As I light the candle for the first night of Hanukkah, I am filled with the feeling of great calm and being centered. At the end of my 'Statement', I write that "I paint the beauty that surrounds me". Always have and always will. I was taught to do all things with love and joy, that has helped me over my many years but especially during this time of Covid-19.

I have to laugh at those that said that artists are non-essential. I do not think anything could be more wrong, especially now. We have a chance with every creation, to express emotion and show others our prospective. We help others understand and be aware of what is possible. We create as a reflection of ourselves, our community and the world. Our experiences help others to understand their own experiences. Hell, we can even make their living rooms look better!

But the best is seeing others being so clever in ways that they have changed and reinvented themselves. Through social media, I am so encouraged, seeing friends and strangers knitting, baking and cooking, Painting By Numbers, redecorating and even writing. And their first attempts are really good! It makes me so happy to see people create to enhance their own lives. It has a ripple effect. It makes the world more beautiful and that is very essential.

Website: debbigreen.com
facebook.com/debbigreen
instagram.com/debbi_green

Michael McCall

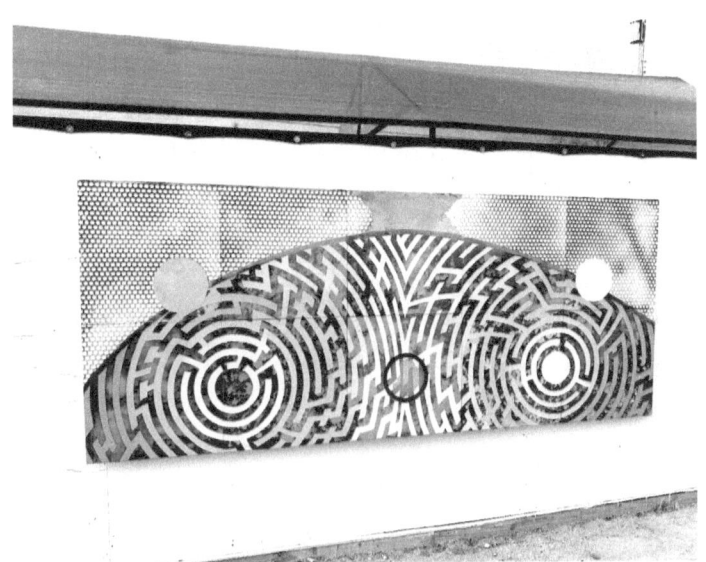

Name: Michael McCall
Discipline: Painter
Country: United States of America

EXPECTATIONS & LOSS

The 2020 shutdown due to the Covid-19 pandemic is unprecedented in our time. Somehow, all the momentum we had created and followed in an attempt to "keep up" has evaporated. Our desire to show up for everything in support of our colleagues, to view their talents, has now been limited to turning on a computer and experiencing a digital exhibit, a music performance, or a zoom meeting while staying in place at home. It's a relief to not have to travel across town continually to 'show up', but the lack of social contact is sorely missed by. This isolation may not change much in the near future as the virus among us continues, as does the ever-present fear.

Three years ago I left Los Angeles in hopes of a simpler life; to live in a rural area of the Mojave Desert. Luckily, I landed an exciting job of curating and directing the exhibitions at the Yucca Valley Visual & Performing Arts Center. So much for that simpler life…the parent company had big ideals, but very little experience in the machinations of the art world. That was ok with me, I got to design the arts center's offerings to a hungry public. The job introduced me to the artists of the greater Joshua Tree area communities which cover a 60-mile area from Morongo Valley eastward out to Wonder Valley, California. The excitement was contagious within the arts community. This was going to be a big time, state-of-the-art space in which I could champion the talents of the local art community, along with my desire to include regional, national and international artists as well.

To support and pay homage to the local artistic community, I built the first two exhibitions to include over 60 artists, first paying tribute to famed artist Noah Purifoy, and to the wonderful assemblage art created in the desert. These exhibitions were huge, they put us on the map with a splash, and the expectations increased. Our mission statement along with the over-the-top features promised on our website, very few which were put into effect during the first year, led to some disappointment within the arts community. The parent company, the Hi-Desert

Cultural Center, seemed robust and alive. I like everyone else, thought their finances were solid, as the community witnessed the renovation of a 15,000 square foot facility like no other in southern California. I suggested numerous times that hiring a professional arts-grants writer would garner the financial support for the programming I was planning. The HDCC chose not to do this, why I am not sure, but that was a big mistake. Two years into the programming and into our 9th major exhibition, the forced closure due to Covid-19 hit March 13, 2020. Appropriately, it was Friday the 13th.

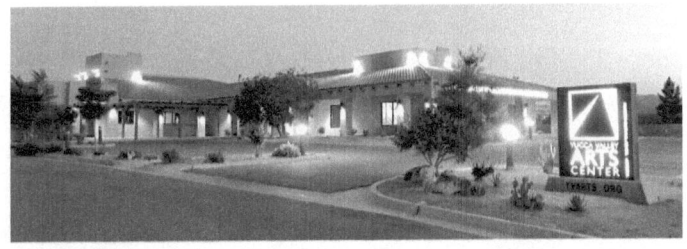

Even before the pandemic, the support from the local community and especially the art-buying public was lacking. From the very beginning I attempted to convince the HDCC board that art sales would not finance our huge endeavor. The real question is how do you continue to operate a brick and mortar facility for the public to have a real experience in viewing artworks, especially now with the closures? I have heard that online sales are improving since the shutdown, allowing galleries to hopefully stay in business. Many commercial art galleries are trying to open by appointments-only, trying to keep staff and audience safe during Covid. This has eliminated the way the public viewed art by just showing up, walking into a gallery and browsing a show, maybe a few in a single afternoon. Is this how we will progress for the next few years, with opening nights of exhibitions eliminated, art fairs across the world either cancelled or delayed, art conferences online, and social contact within arts communities all cancelled due to this pandemic? Shutting down a non-profit facility like ours for 8 months to a year is a death nail. I imagine this is the case for most smaller galleries, arts centers like ours, and many higher-education art galleries. The economy within the arts community is struggling to stay afloat. All momentum has been lost.

When the shutdown first occured, it was a relief to get back to focusing on my own work in the studio. Finishing projects that had been suspended while building the arts center felt great at first, but the seriousness of the pandemic coupled with the unrest within the country began to get into my head. I didn't like being told to stay in place so I got on a plane and flew to Chicago, rented a car, and drove back across America. I got back the day George Floyd was murdered. Witnessing the protests and rioting on TV with an election looming in the near distance, made it more difficult to focus in the studio. Each day I would run into the proverbial wall, wondering what was essential, trying to avoid the news, asking myself what was the meaning of all this? The West coast was on fire, smoke filled the sky, it was apocalyptic. I took a day trip into LA and was astonished by the increase in homelessness. I scampered back to the desert and hid out in the studio, expecting the worse. How did I let myself get so messed up by this? The studio was supposed to be calming and therapeutic.

As creative souls, we are sometimes too open and sensitive for the horrors of life. It's a jungle out there. Artists know that solace and reflectiveness comes with spending time in the studio. It is actually our therapy, but is therapy the only value in making an artwork? Are artists supposed to help fix this mess called reality? What ultimately can art accomplish? Kurt Vonnegut once wrote that first, artists cannot fix the entire world, and second, they make one part of it just right! Experiencing art, whether a film, a painting, listening to a piece of music, all these help make life worth living. Without these experiences, what would this life be? The enjoyment and appreciation of witnessing beauty, the endorphins produced, this is all good for us. For my own part, reflecting reality was never my desire. The desire to escape, to find beauty in fantasy, felt more powerful to me. Accidents, disasters and now pandemics are all part of the realignment of our existence, but imagination can construct a new reality, a new escape.

Creating artwork has the ability to embed the unimaginable in material. Creativity is a survival strategy; it's in every bone in our bodies, and always has been. It is based in the unknown. Looking into the void, starring at a blank sheet of paper or a white canvas allows the imagination to roam. There is no formula for making art, it doesn't work that way. You have to trust that crazy moments will occur during the process to trigger the imagination. We are definitely in one of those crazy

moments. The positive spin on the pandemic is that we will get through this, we will return to normal. Really, will we? The damage to the arts, to the freedom of expression and especially to the freedom of experience has been gigantic. I don't think we will go back to anything like normal. The worldwide destruction of markets, the increased poverty around the world, how can this be resolved? Does making another piece of art have any possibility to help, or are we artists just a bunch of self-involved people, trying to make sense of the insanity of the moment? I hope I am completely wrong and that there will be a normalcy that reoccurs, one better with a new sense of selflessness and caring. That will demand our imaginations. I believe we do have that within us to move into another epoch of highly creative souls healing ourselves and the larger populace.
Michael McCall
Nov. 7, 2020

Website: www.michaelmccall.org

Jesse Standlea

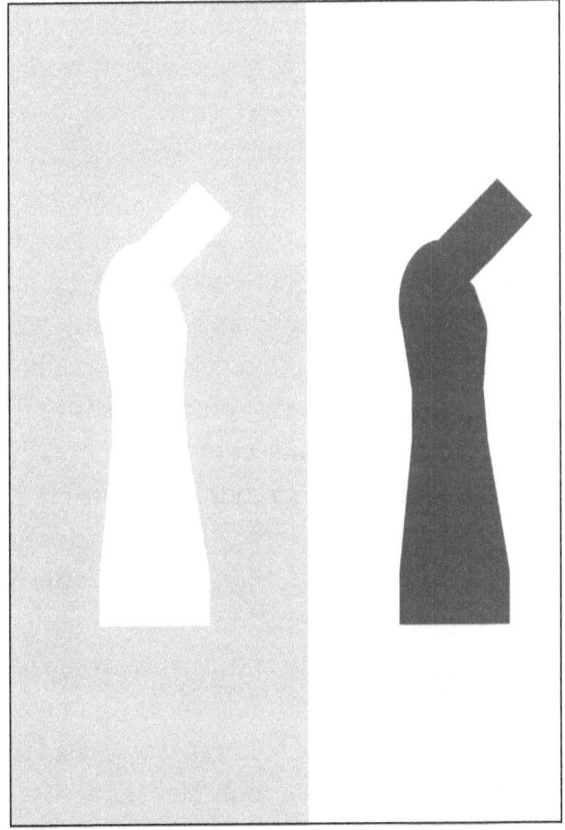

Name: Jesse Standlea
Discipline: Art
Country: United States of America

2020:
Title: 11-21-20

With meditation there is just one thing, you focus on your breath. It is about being fully immersed in the task, just that. No more; there does not need to be anything more. Should you reach an ethereal moment of clarity, bravo, but you would not be able to experience such a revelation by trying, so the beauty of meditation is really in its simplicity. The more complex a task, the more effort, and mastery that is needed to maintain a sense of harmony or to reach flow.

Art and nature are similar. A still image does not need the complexity of a story. To really understand any subject in its whole, in its entirety, is often beyond my comprehension. So one approach the artist often takes is to focus in on particular aspects of a subject or to simplify complexity. Take this hillside scene, on one side there are houses, on the other is a nature preserve. If I want to emphasize my connection with nature, I will simplify out the houses. Placing me in a nature reserve on a hillside path. I look out at the picturesque scene and it reminds me of a still life painting. If I were to add movement or animation, it would need to be subtle, the stillness would need to come first. Only then could I bring in motion, and that motion would enter along the upper third of a fixed part of this horizontal picture plane.

Hmm. I think to myself as I walk up to the crest of my local hills. I live inland from the ocean but there are a few spots where the hills break and one can see the ocean harbor. These were the types of conversations I would have with my friend Kiffy. Perhaps he would then erupt with vigor and say "What are people doing, don't they know we are all going to die!" His vigor could be ignited by societal differences in opinion, or his desire to help those who have less. You see Kiffy had worked for a short time in Kenya and would speculate, "I think in the future people will think, that was crazy that we spent our money buying $80,000 cars when we could have been helping out starving people". He once said if you are born in America, your quality of living is historically higher than kings in the past. He would emphasize dentists, with an elevated "Entists." And it is true not having access to modern dental care or proper sanitation for that matter can be life-threatening. And so can our mental state.

As I come to a fork in the road, I opt not for the ocean view, but for a longer walk. As I look out over the hills, I think of James Turell and his ability to have this magical effect of changing the color of the sky by focusing us on what's around it.

There is stillness to this landscape, and for short moments it feels like it is a still life painting, but just for a moment. While there is that stillness things are slowly yet constantly in motion. The land is constantly evolving and shifting, there is the damper of the light over time. The sky can seem like all the filters are turned up after a storm and while I find beauty in these snapshots and in the way the light hits the grasses that spring out of the land, my construct of beauty is in part based on how these elements shift to fit and function in their environment. The space and time always linking them together. In that sense finding beauty in nature is an illusion, yet the more I think about its complexity the further I get from that pure connection, a connection to the land, where things seem to click and the world might even play to you.

Along the trail, looking out on the reserve, are small tables that have A-frame roofs. As I arrive at one I take a seat on top of the table to meditate. If I look back from where I came, I can see another one off in the distance along the path had I taken the ocean view direction. I close my eyes and start by focusing on my breath. Silence. After a time, I open my eyes to a stormy yet vivid landscape. The wind blows over the grasses which are now brightly saturated earth tones. I look out on this picture, and the land's stillness is there with the exception of a couple of horses moving as if in slow motion along the crest of the hill. Something about those grasses against the sky makes me think of a Roland Reiss flower painting. Well, a Roland Reiss' flower painting without the flowers might create enough visual tension mixed with a sense of mystery to represent the conversations I had with Kiffy.

You see Kiffy took his own life. While he did not believe in god there was a spirituality he carried with himself. It would be a mistake to call him a spiritual person but he had an ineffable presence. There was India, Alaska, Africa and his meditation retreats. When looking at the stars, there was endless curiosity, "What is beyond the end of the universe?" he asked the speaker at a lecture we attended at Griffith Observatory titled "The End." In conceptualizing nothing and then there being a big something, his curiosity couldn't hold him back from wondering what is the playing field I am imagining this occurrence within.

In the construction of form, shapes combine to create more complex shapes and in theory, they are on a plane. The magic trick is that you are so focused on the shapes on a plane that you don't bother worrying about that space beyond where the plane exists. We were once looking at the Milky Way on a lake that we had arrived at having paddled out to from a smaller lake. It was seeing the curve of the Milky Way that touched me. That night I first had the thought that if I don't know where my consciousness started then I don't know that I didn't have consciousness before I was alive. Having talked about the existential dilemma with Kiffy, that moment gave me a sense of peace while opening the dialogue that there might be more to this story. Seeing the curve of the galaxy allowed me to conceptualize an existence where I did not know its start and where I sure don't know its end. It was his love of and capacity to marvel at life and things science that gave our conversations an element I would call spiritual.

I get up and walk along the path. I decide to take my shoes off and let my feet touch the ground. Feeling the physical connection to the land, I think through conversations with Kiffy, where place and time have different rules. In those memoirs, there is at times the feeling of how things were, an escape from the shock, from that phone call in which I heard those unimaginable words. "Kiffy killed himself."

Place and time affect perception as many have noticed this year. My recounting memories of conversations was perhaps the largest perceptual anchor during the lockdown, in contrast to visiting physical spaces like the trip to Mountain View, a town that seemed a ghost version of a reality I once knew. Driving through town I felt like I was there and not there at the same time. The town and the house were foggy almost as if grey washed.

For a second the color seemed to come back as I drove up to his house, I saw the family cars parked in the driveway and for that moment I thought everyone was home. I had forgotten why I was actually there. Reality quickly came back washing away the color. I had come to help go through some of his items and pick up one of his bikes that had been gifted to me. Walking into his house was like walking in on a life frozen in time. The bikes were all out like they had recently been used, one looked like it was being worked on, and one bike still had one of Kiffy's workout shirts on it, helmet attached. To touch anything almost felt like trespassing on a family moment frozen in time.

I will remember seeing framed pictures of the Lewis and Clark expedition heading west. I think he would want to be remembered having traveled west, while he didn't talk about it much I think he romanticized the notion.

I will remember seeing his bird-watching scope, it was out lying flat on the dining room table. It's that space where I can distinctly remember times with him in vivid color, that was now a hazy grey. At the intersection of that desaturation of color is the memory, giving him a hug for the last time. It's strange how those two distinctly different realities could now occupy the same space, but duality is often in my thoughts.

I take one last look out onto the vast stillness of the landscape, before taking the path curving down the backside of the hillcrest that will wind and eventually lead me home. This looks like the west, a view of open land. Living here my whole life I suppose I never thought of this being the west, it is just here.

So who was Kiffy to me? He was the voice I often had in my head when figuring out a work or life matter. Artists often carry voices from their professors, or mentors using this to simulate conversations and to work through artistic decisions. Roland Reiss' voice comes to me as the guru, while Kiffy's voice is one of reason and the friend that always has your best interests at heart. He was a person who was inspiring to his peers. As a teacher, he reminded us that the world is an amazing place and that it takes effort to remind ourselves of that.

Taking a seat on my porch with a hot cup of tea and writing on my iPad, I look at the hills and write.

11-21-20

Kiffy is the person that will continue to help me as I keep this journal for my own health and wellness. I set off today on my walk as part of a commitment to putting health first in my life, where I will center my thinking, my actions, and my creative output. There was something about meditation that was important to Kiffy and is becoming an important part of my life now. That and my walks, but let's not overcomplicate things.

Website: http://www.standlea.com

Remembering:
Christopher Purvis Aka "Kiffy"
Mountain View CA, Passed on April 7, 2020.

John Dingler

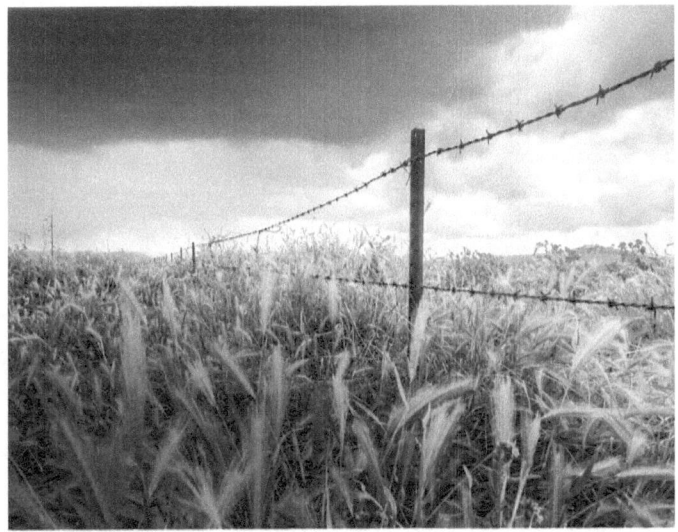

Name: John Dingler
Discipline: Artist
Country: United States of America

I met Hank, a bottle and cans collector, across the street from my art studio on my way to the adjacent Smart & Final downtown LA, CA. He said that he makes from $150 to $200/day on his collection route, a 20 mile walk pushing a shopping cart. It had seven large black trash bags nearly bursting with product tied up to the front, top, and rear. Two small ones protruded from each side. I offered $10 to photograph him in my studio to which he readily agreed. We had a difficult time wrangling the cart through the studio entrance door. I took many photos, different poses, with and without the cart. I situated him before my recently-completed eight foot high graphite drawing. We shared our histories and interests. He declined the $10; I guess he felt wealthy enough.

Website: http://www.johndinglerart.com

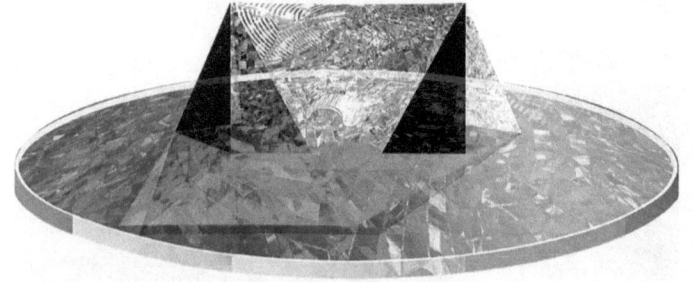

Robert A Costanza

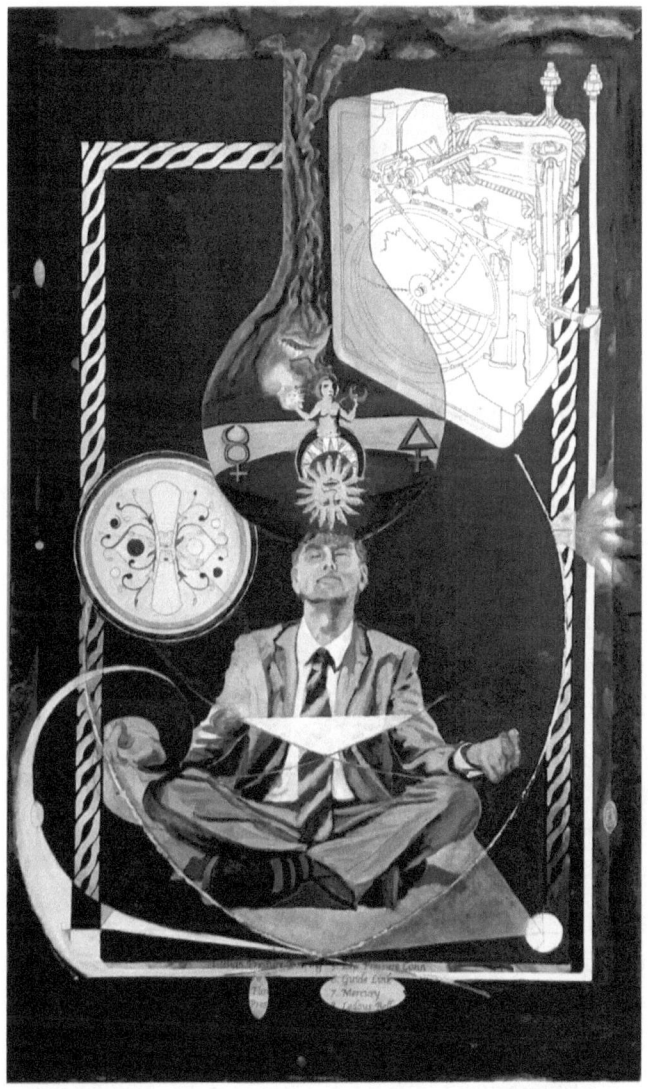

Name: Robert A Costanza
Discipline: Artist
Country: United States of America

2020:
The Year to Forget - 2020
by Robert Costanza

For the entire fall preceding 2020, I was enrolled in an intense, three-month writing course hosted by a very popular online magazine. I had invested a lot of money in the course and it was actually quite fun. Students from all over the world gathered online in a weekly Zoom class, and we had smaller, subgroup meetings where we read each other's articles and gave feedback, updates, rewrites, and then more feedback. There was also an active Facebook page for input from fellow students. This all led to submitting polished articles to the online magazine. Besides wanting to dive deep and explore the craft of writing, I was hoping to grow my business. Potentially, millions of readers could link to my company from an author bio.

We were required to write five articles. Each time I pushed "submit," my hopes soared—the editing staff would seek an exclusive contract after reading this! Actually, magazine editors proceeded to chew apart my masterpieces. They seemed to be seeking not elaborately crafted articles, rather, cute little sound bites that would present well to a dumbed down demographic. I cut, rewrote, restructured as suggested but without dumbing down my content too much. In the end, not one article was published. This brought me up to New Year's Eve when I got food poisoning. Welcome to 2020.

Artist, ART, & Story: A Moment in Time, 2020: International

Once I regained a tiny bit of momentum, I realized the importance of finding a creative avenue to travel. I set about crafting portable meditation benches from exotic woods I had been collecting. It was quite a learning curve, especially with all the stains, wood sealers, and varnishes. Along the way, I had my prototype benches photographed and set about updating my website with the new products.

By this time it was late February and I had a good selection of benches, so I set up my vendor's tent in the back yard and started working on displays for the new store. I planned to travel to festivals and farmer's markets in spring/summer 2020. I was excited for an entirely new store with paintings and handcrafted wood items in addition to all the packs and silk-screened T-shirts I create. I was signed up at a slew of venues, investing thousands in entry fees. Wanting to go further up the West Coast, I also started upgrading my Sprinter van with solar panels so I could have a refrigerator and some other conveniences on the road.

This was the time frame that the LOCKDOWN hit; I was just at the point of starting back at the outdoor markets. Spending fall/winter in the studio creating products, I naturally turn outwards in spring/summer to be around happy people in marketplaces. It's the payoff I receive for isolating over the colder months. But now I was being asked to isolate just as spring was blooming.

I turned my attention to a slew of unfinished paintings I had in process, turned my rental room into a painting studio, and set to work. Just a week into this creative flow, I was served an eviction notice. The live-in property manager was starting to realize the life of an artist isn't a nine-to-five job. I actually expected to cook meals in the kitchen, my room was an art studio, there was sawdust in the back yard. It was too much for her apparently. I knew the eviction laws (I think all artists are familiar with them) and there was a moratorium, but the manager's escalating drama became too much, and I vacated to the Sprinter van.

I was able to continue painting in the Sprinter as I turned my attention to the process of moving back to my real room, which I had been avoiding. Extremely toxic people had moved onto the property. I couldn't fully clear out, as I was protecting a dear old man, Doc, who was declining into dementia and to whom I owed so much. I refused to allow these characters to be part of his life for long, so I never vacated my room on Docs' property. I started moving items back into my room for the transition back, spending nights painting, and sleeping off the property in the Sprinter so I could maintain a creative flow.

In short order, I was assaulted and my tires were slashed; I became entangled in a war I did not want. With the eviction moratorium there was little we could do, so I retreated to create at campsites, when those were not shut down due to Covid-19. I would visit the property weekly and do battle, console the others who were being traumatized, and cook and be with Doc. Soon enough, one of the two toxic people (they were a couple), was driven from the property. Unfortunately, the guy promptly took over her room while still occupying his room. Their unpaid rent had piled up over six months and there was no end in sight.

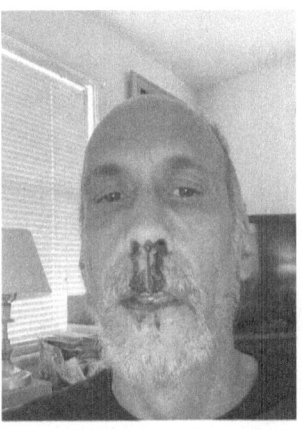

Realizing I did not have the skills to deal with this situation, I offered my room to a dear friend who had skills and who loved Doc dearly. He moved in, and I vacated to a family member's place further north, who happened to have a lot of work required to fix up dilapidated shop areas. So, the summer wore on. The diesel Sprinter broke down, and I became a diesel mechanic for two months while also rearranging, organizing, and culling an extensive array of wood and metal shop equipment and tools. It wasn't far from creativity, I was working with my hands, but I was not painting, I was not running my business — all my events were cancelled and the money refunded. I worked onwards in what life had presented to me.

Then an opportunity came along. Normally, I substitute teach for income, but that was out due to COVID. I received a call from someone who needed my engineering skills as a consultant. I was able to do this work remotely; I just had to get back to Los Angeles for a week and get the ball rolling. A day before leaving, I was in the shop when a large railroad tie slid from its precarious angle right onto my foot, fracturing a bone. 2020 just entered its final chapter—fall was here.

I drove to LA with a purple, swollen foot and appeared at the job site limping with a cane. The week I spent in LA was the hottest on record, with temperatures peaking at 120 degrees Fahrenheit at the test lab where I was working. It was a tough period as the injury did not allow me to engage in my daily yoga practice, and as I got further from that, even my meditation hours wound down to zero. Soon I was swimming in a sea of misery. I am being dramatic here to illustrate how I become when not doing my practices! For the first time in the year I had really crashed, content to knock out consulting hours, eat, and scroll Netflix videos. No creativity flow whatsoever.

Back in the Bay Area, I finished up the consulting and wrapped up work on the properties I had been engaged in through the summer and fall. By this time, my foot had healed enough so I was able to do some yoga and light hiking. I used these efforts to nurse back creative inspiration. Back at my home, the toxic guy had accepted a multi-thousand-dollar payment to clear off the property. My friend worked to clear piles and piles of items and debris that the toxic couple had brought onto the property. I proceeded to run an ad for a care-worker and, incredibly, we found a perfect fit.

Christmas week, I returned home to a peaceful, zen-like atmosphere. Doc was happy, the caretaker ecstatic with her luck for landing in such a beautiful home in Ojai, California, with free rent in trade for feeding a sweet, dear man. I used the last week of 2020 to put the finishing touches on the one painting that was a hundred percent completed in 2020, pictured at the beginning of this story.

Website: https://www.rocketbuddha.com/

Our Ever Changing World: Through the Eyes of Artists: Book 14

Mary-Gail King

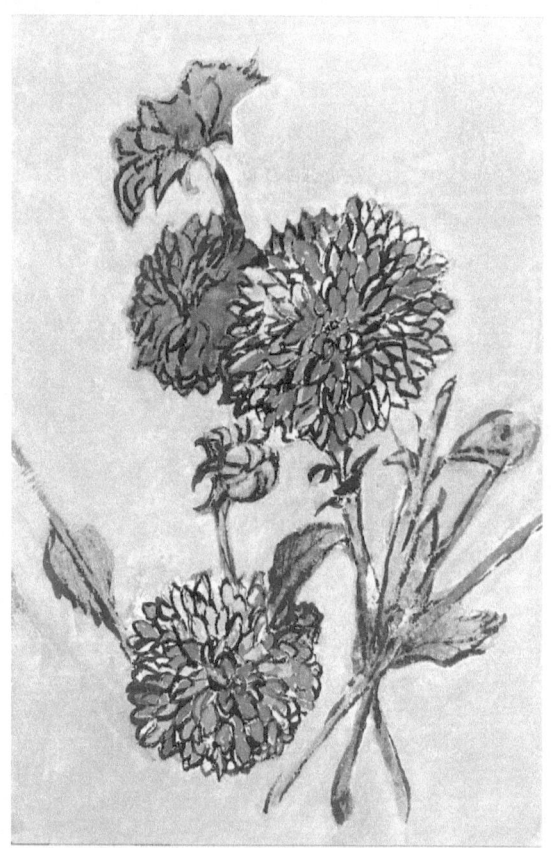

Name: Mary-Gail King
Discipline: Painter
Country: United States of America

2020:
Wednesday, March 17 or maybe it was Thursday, March 18, 2020 I got home late. It was around mid-night. I rolled into bed and picked up my phone. It was a habit

I couldn't seem to break. If I turn out the light and put my pillow under my head in a particular way my body will probably remember the months and years I did this as I watched what seemed like a moral free fall taking place in our country.

The news cycle gave me whiplash and I couldn't look away. I became secretly compulsive about watching the evening news which had me tossing and turning on a regular basis.

That particular night I checked the headlines and saw that the state of California had just ordered a mandatory lockdown. I was exhausted after a long day of teaching and filming some projects I was working on. Tired as I was, I forced myself to get up out of bed and go to the nearest all night grocery store to stock up.

I bought ten cans of tomatoes for $10. How could I pass that up? I tossed three cans of tuna into my cart channeling my mother who always kept extra canned food in our pantry in case of disaster. I even bought a fifty pound bag of flour and yeast. I've used all but two cans of the tomatoes. The three cans of tuna are in the back of the pantry. The flour has been gone for months. It's March 1, 2021 tomorrow. I was carb loading.

Back to that first night, I remember being grateful to get home without getting pulled over by the local police. I had seen them strategically parked at various times leading up to this. I had no idea, nor did anyone, what was coming.

Once I got settled in, the days and weeks blurred together. I discovered that all I wanted to do was shrink into the studio I created at home. When I wasn't curled up at home I went for hikes. I watched the news as disaster after disaster crossed the planet. I'd like to note I've stopped watching the news and have substituted a wide array of Netflix and Amazon movies instead. That's positive.

As I shrank into a small world, I traveled only as far as my new hiking shoes would take me. And I reached out to the larger world virtually in ways I never had before. Thank God for the internet. I wasn't alone.

I wasn't desperate, but I knew I had to figure out how to work from home. I reached out to my students and collectors through Zoom and social media. I obsessively watched late night tv hungry for news and humor. I was fascinated as I watched Stephen Colbert, Ellen, the two late night Jimmys and James Corden in their living rooms, garages, and basements. They used technology available to all of us to transform their couches and extra bedrooms into video production studios.

I could do that. So I hooked up my iPhone over a 5"x7" pad of paper, set up my computer so I could talk to people on camera, got a Zoom account, and started painting. Talking and painting work for me. The piece I've included for this book is one of hundreds of little sketches I've done of whatever was in front of me. In this case it was dahlias.

I'm lucky to live in a small community on a university campus. The campus is surrounded by a combination of mountainous backcountry and farmland. So I walked. I also obsessively created course content, often on the walks, and worked to promote what I do in order to move my art classes online.

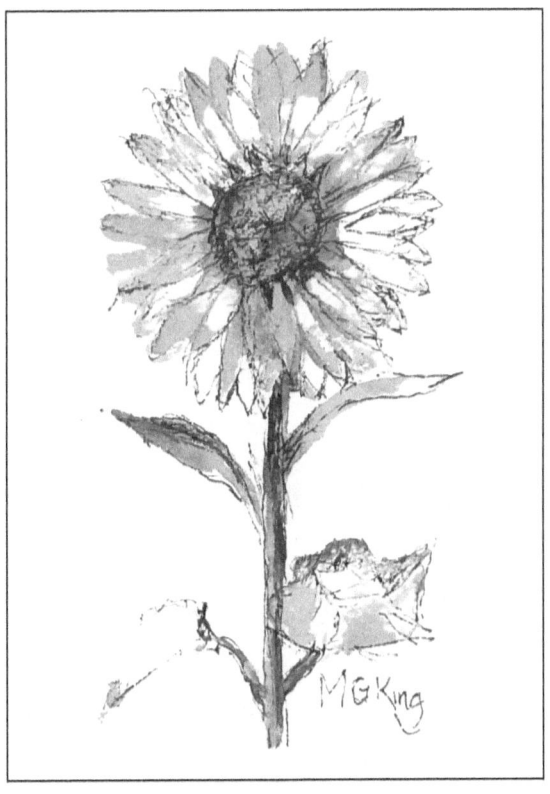

I did live feeds of myself sketching in lemon orchards and took my friends on virtual walks as I talked about the shadows and textures of the grasses by the roadside. I took poetry books on my treks and sketched mountains on the blank pages between poems.

Quarantine forced me to focus. I had to move quickly to keep my business going. So I did what is easy for me, to paint, in order to achieve what seemed hard at the time, to make money online and secure a solid future for myself.

If this is a hero's journey it's far from over. The story has a clear beginning. We're in the middle. Who knows how it will end.

We've changed but we can't see exactly what will come of this yet. That will take some time and, if the past is any indicator, there will be a plot twist or two.

As this has unfolded a few things have become clear to me.

I don't fail. I'm resilient and can adapt to just about anything.

I'm a good artist and an excellent teacher. I have some things to learn about technology.

I'm a really good businesswoman. I felt like a bit of imposter before this but I have money in the bank and it's still coming in. One of the most amusing things I did was get a thirty year Economic Impact Disaster Loan. I was grateful and will be 90 when I finally pay it off!

The world takes me seriously. As story after story has come out I've learned that my situation is similar to millions of other small business owners. And we are so much more important than I ever realized.

My people and community believe in me and we all love each other deeply.

I am fortunate that I can stay at home and be healthy. Not everyone can. Many people have food insecurity, are behind on rent or house payments. A record number of women have quit their jobs because children are schooling from home. There will be long term fallout from those things.

I have advantages many people in the world don't have. I am a white college educated woman who is well connected and has considerably more resources than I ever suspected.

I have learned to be grateful for everything and everyone in my life.

I had better enjoy this life. The past year it seemed as if every day new things happened that required major adjustments. Uncertainty has been the norm. I couldn't plan ahead the way I like to. And I learned I'd better be ok with that. Life is far too beautiful.

This story is far from unique. I have fit neatly into a pocket of history with billions of other people. So this extraordinary event has become a shared new way of being.
I'll keep you posted. Who knows how this will work out. Until the next plot twist I'm signing off.

Website: http://www.marygailking.com

Our Ever Changing World: Through the Eyes of Artists: Book 14

Kayla Cloonan

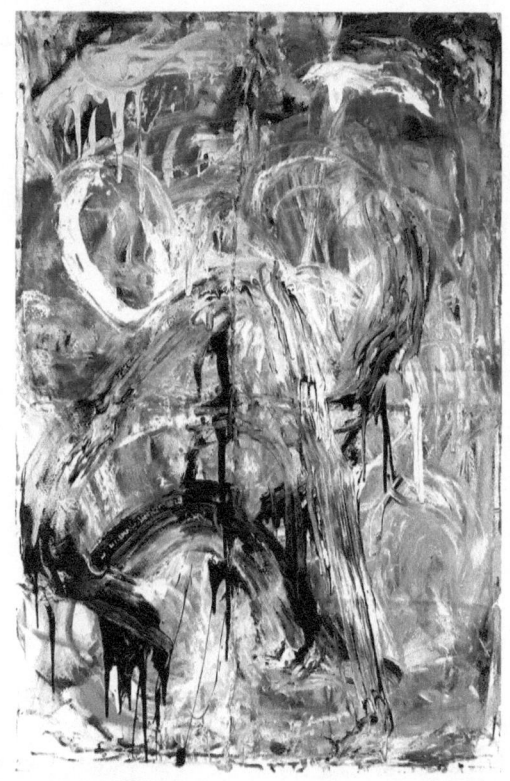

Name: Kayla Cloonan
Discipline: Interdisiplinary Artist
Country: United States of America

2020:
Going Blindly Into the Future
by Kayla L. Cloonan

Many times and yet here I stand. On the precipice of a new chapter in life.

I liked it when you went to work and I could have time to myself. The words of my partner, now ex, four months after quarantine had begun for us. Never a good sign. We were both laid off our respective food service jobs as a result of the global COVID-19 pandemic making it's way to Los Angeles and the United States at large. Just before the stay at home order was put in place for California, I suggested the lay offs to my boss. I figured at least we could apply for unemployment. Sure as shit after my last day there, the complex that housed the coffee shop I worked at shutdown. Someone tested positive at one of the corporate offices in the business complex.

I'm not gonna lie, after the initial shock of change I was thrilled at the idea of being essentially a full-time studio artist. It started out invigorating. Being that my partner was a musician, we each had our creative projects to keep us busy. But as the days turned into weeks and then months, the feeling of isolation started to set in along with the financial instability. My therapist told me not to future fantasize, so I planned my days as they came, writing on my to-do-lists what I thought I could accomplish in a single day. The impending sense of doom came and went as I finished more studio projects than any previous year. The world seemingly crumbled around us, the numbers continuing to rise. I only left the apartment for groceries, cigarettes and liquor. And the occasional espresso coffee drink with a vegan chocolate donut.

With no weekends to compare to weeks, the days melted into each other. The only thing keeping me going was art.

And the next bottle of whiskey. Now mind you, I'm an alcoholic. Have been since damn near the first sip back in my early 20's. I've known for a while but without having a job to justify my functionality, it came to the forefront. The cravings varied – triggers being anything from stress and depression to evening boredom. A few weeks of struggling hard to have 'just one drink', waking up mid afternoon hungover, slowly losing the resistance to fantasizing of the future and one black-out night that left my partner less than pleased to be around me, I realized I needed to quit. I needed to wake up early and catch that quiet moment just before lawn mowers started revving and music began blaring out of open apartment windows in the mid-summer heat. I needed a new routine to replace the old work schedule. Something that needed my attention everyday.

I stopped drinking, started grinding coffee the night before, having a cup of coffee with a cigarette before breakfast and taking a shower every morning. In favor of a daily never-ending project, I decided to grow plants. I'd never grown anything before, at least not successfully. But with some soil, seeds and internet research, I began my garden. I liked the sound of that. My Garden.

As far as the outside world knew, I was doing fine. Fantastic even. I was posting online about new art, cooking, bread baking and my garden just about everyday. The only person who knew what went on behind the curtain was my partner and our relationship suffered for it. It was made worse by the fact that he wasn't an addict and therefore couldn't fully understand how hard it was for me to resist walking just three blocks to the liquor store.

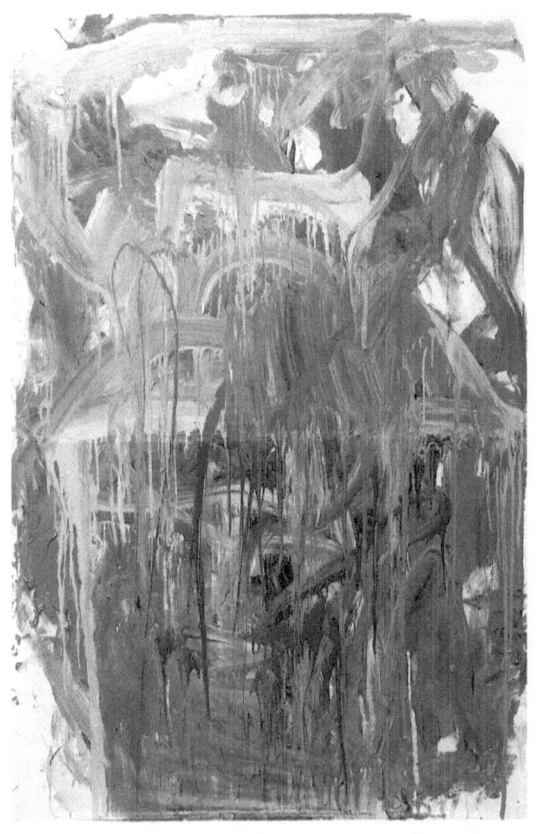

By the end of July it became increasingly clear that neither of us would be able to continue to afford housing costs and we decided it would be best if we moved in with his parents up in northern California. It was a tough decision and a nightmare trying to find moving vehicles to rent. Turns out we weren't the only ones moving out of the city. Like many times before in my life, I had to decide what unused studio supplies to abandon, what finished artwork to throw away, what leftover hopes and dreams to seal up in empty booze boxes gifted to me by the owner of the local liquor store. We were close friends by then. I always bought my cigarettes from him, even though they were 25 cents more a pack than at the 7-eleven. Gotta keep those local shops going somehow. He always made sure to order the whiskey I liked and in sobriety stocked extra flavors of the kombucha which became my replacement beverage of choice.

Saying goodbye to the apartment meant more to me than just leaving a living space. It meant giving up independence and there's nothing I hold onto stronger.

The drive up there wasn't too bad. My cat didn't seem to mind being in the car. When we got there we discovered that the U-haul building near the house didn't have storage units. My partner had failed to mention to me that the neighborhood was so bad that if you kept a U-haul or even a car with visible stuff in it on the street, it would be broken into. After eight hours of traveling, we ended up unloading the entirety of the moving truck and both our cars into a storage space almost an hour out of town. We didn't eat dinner that night.

After nearly 3 months sober, it didn't take long for the misery of being cooped up in someone else's house in the middle of an unfamiliar neighborhood for me to find the nearest liquor store. Admittedly, I had researched ahead of the move and it was the only store of any kind within walking distance. Less than a week of being there and

I had another black-out night. The next morning, my partner asked me to leave. There were few verbal exchanges after that conversation. I didn't bother to ask what had transpired the night before; I knew it must have been bad.

Hungover as can be, that very same day I packed up all my things from the room, went to the storage unit and fit as much of my belongings as I could into my Jeep.

Once again like many times before, I parted with art and supplies. I had to abandon a mattress my partner and I purchased together as well as a brand new mini-fridge I'd purchased myself just before the move. I made the embarrassing phone call to my Mom who informed me of a 2hr long Facetime call we'd had the night before, none of which I remembered. It was okay for me to come home, she said. It didn't feel okay to me. I even reached out to a friend in my old LA neighborhood seeing if there was a vacancy in her house. Of course there wasn't, but deep down I knew regardless that it was time for me to be with family again. It had been 7 years since I lived anywhere near family. I was the only one on the west coast.

By 6pm that day I had the car packed and the cat ready for travel. With a lame patting hug from my ex and an insincere wish of luck, I started toward the highway alone. But I had my cat, I told myself. I wasn't alone.

It was the fourth time I drove cross-country but my first time solo. I was nervous starting out but the trip ended up being unbelievably cathartic. The long hours of driving were tough and a little boring at times, but every time I talked to my cat she lifted her little head up inside the cat bag and looked right at me as if to say she was okay and then in turn, I was okay. I stopped whenever I wanted to, whether it was for more caffeine, to use the restroom or to stay at a hotel, four of which I stayed at throughout the trip. Nothing quite like a hot shower and the chance to be horizontal. Waking up at 4am for an early morning drive became an invigorating routine on the trip. Few people on the road for the first few hours.

My cat loved the hotels! She sure kept me busy – I always had to set everything up ahead of time – the litter-box and food and check to make sure there were no random spots for her to get stuck. The first place we stayed, I had to pull the whole bed-frame away from the wall because she managed to find a little space to hide when she clearly wasn't too thrilled to get back in the car again. She's a curious explorer, just like me, so no space was was left unexamined. All in all she did well and I did too.

Arriving back in my hometown was strange. It had been over 2 years since I'd even visited. I always made a point to try and meet my Mom during her business trips, avoiding the state of Florida entirely. Some things had changed, but over all it looked familiar. The pond we used to go to as kids was still there but the tree we used to swing on a rope from was cut down to a stump. The grocery store I started working at when I was 16 was still there but it was filled with new faces, few of which I recognized. No-one recognized me. Maybe it was the mask, maybe it was the tattoos, maybe it was the thick skin I'd grown all the years of having the sweetness beaten out of me. I was different, but somehow still the same. I was still me, no matter how much I'd changed. I welcomed the humidity; the frogs and stick bugs and palmetto bushes. I felt strange, but I also felt free.

Website: https://kaylalcloonan.com/

Our Ever Changing World: Through the Eyes of Artists: Book 14

Edwin Nutting

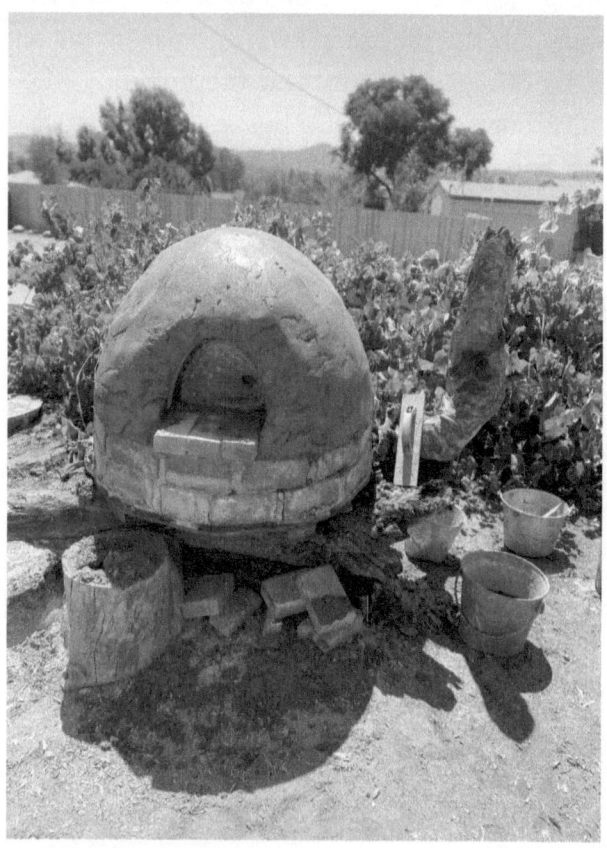

Name: Edwin Nutting
Discipline: Illustrator
Country: United States of America

'Mud Oven'
We are beekeepers, so when some friends from 29 Palms texted they had a colony of bees in their barn/painting studio we agreed to remove them. It's a pleasant 3 hour

drive from Bostonia in San Diego County through the Anza-Borrego into the Colorado then Mojave deserts, an amazing drive. On arrival it was feasible to remove rather than destroy the colony, 90 minutes later the Bees were in a file box and ready for the drive home. Before we left we had a tour of their beautiful Home/Studio/Art Residency .. this house & barn originally was a milking operation in the 1920's and turned dump in the 70's... years of clean up resulted in a unique Art building-block tied into 29 Palms as part of the community not just a studio...a neat place to "be here now"... well... we went around the corner and in front of me was a 'Earth Oven' Anna & Ted had built.. still warm from a firing the day before.... I was speechless, I've seen gold in streams....same feeling... it was unexpected and unavoidable my reaction to this radiant beast. I had to build one. We got the Bees home safe and planning for the oven began.

My neighbor had a 60 year old Eucaliptus trunk and roots in his back yard they unearthed.. The way it was shaped..the way it looked.. I thought it would be a good addition to the front yard, we got his Bobcat tractor and maneuvered this 2,000# chunk of wood down the street and up my driveway onto my front yard.. so there it sat until I came home with the oven idea...it looked like it might support 2 more tons of material if set and cut right. I flipped the burl until it's balance seemed natural, grabbed the chainsaw and cut a level notch in her 5' wide and 30" off the ground.. for the next 2 months I invested my soul and body to this project, collecting bricks, buying sand and mixing with my bare feet these combinations of layers to get her into position of taking charge of the fires within to be.

Website: www.nuttingairbrushgallery.com

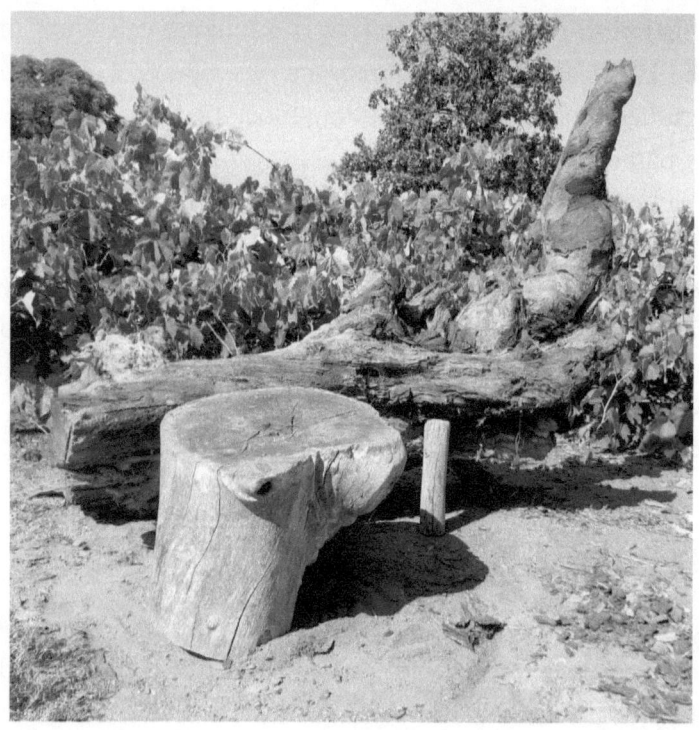

Nancy Good

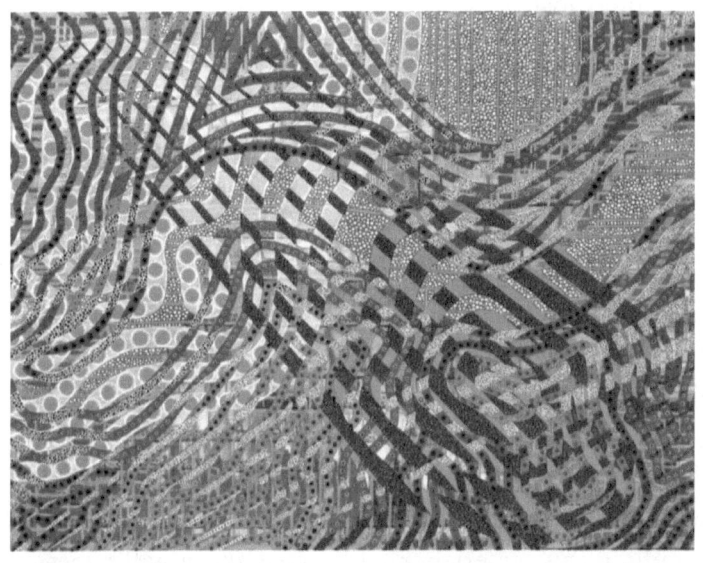

Name: Nancy Good
Discipline: Conceptual Abstract/Mixed-media
Country: United States of America

Talismanic Solace and Blessing
During Rites of Passage and Diminished Human Contact
by Nancy Good

"Living History" ... this is what many people, from all walks of life, are already calling this unusual time in our world-wide, collective human experience. Pandemic, riots, protests, human rights abuses, violent political and religious divides, climate and environmental upheaval, economic collapse for those most at risk, while the rich and powerful simply get more rich and more powerful ... the world's entire population is affected by at least one, but most often almost all of them collectively. How do I respond? How do I thrive? How do I rise above? How do I sustain hope? What do I grasp onto for solace and even blessing?

In light of these extraordinary events, there are patterns unfolding that indicate our civilization is at a critical juncture in a collective rite of passage where I must move into new awareness in order to thrive (or even survive) as an individual. This important juncture is most often experienced as personal epiphanies followed by growth, but close observation points to this being a collective experience by humanity as a whole. Individually, I see some handling this experience with grace and a willingness to learn through it, while others fight tooth and nail to oppose the evolution that is already progressing with the force of a nuclear reaction. I consider our species at a state of critical mass, so to speak, with regards to collective awareness and memory of what was, what is and what may be. Add to this the pandemic imperatives that limit person-to-person contact for health and well-being, it is no wonder I am floundering and confused as I seek to reconcile my individual desire for normalcy against the collective awareness of what I may have to give up to in order for humanity to flourish again. This state of awareness can be frightening. It can also be transformative. Paintings entitled "Liminal Planes" and "Liminal Planes II" express my observations with regard to a collective rite of passage. Varied layers, even 3D assemblage, seem at first to create a cacophony of visual confusion. However, upon deeper study, divergent planes eventually find unity through elements meant to express the common needs I believe we have as human beings, such as companionship, shelter, purpose, safety, food, protection, love.

Those who have studied physics understand that critical mass is needed to sustain nuclear reaction. I cannot help but apply this concept to the nuclear reaction of necessary changes we are seeing today. We each will remember many things, but we won't all remember them the same way. This does not mean another's memory is invalid. The strength (and critical mass) that comes from weaving all these memories into a collective cord is what is needed for the sake of humanity. I can imagine that other artists feel much the same, as if we're recording time, with an almost desperate necessity, weaving strands of non-linear memories with threads of current events and new awareness. And, it is our collective memory of past and present that will sustain the forward momentum needed to propel us through these challenging times. One recent painting created in response to this is entitled "The Critical Mass of Collective Memory." It visually expresses the density of joining together not only my various individual memories over time and space, but also weaving them with the vastly different memories others may have with regard to what I think are the same experiences. This weaving, through paint and other mark-making, attempts to honor the memories of another, even if I may not have those same memories. By maintaining contact with the memories of another, even if we cannot be in physical contact, I believe we can sustain change.

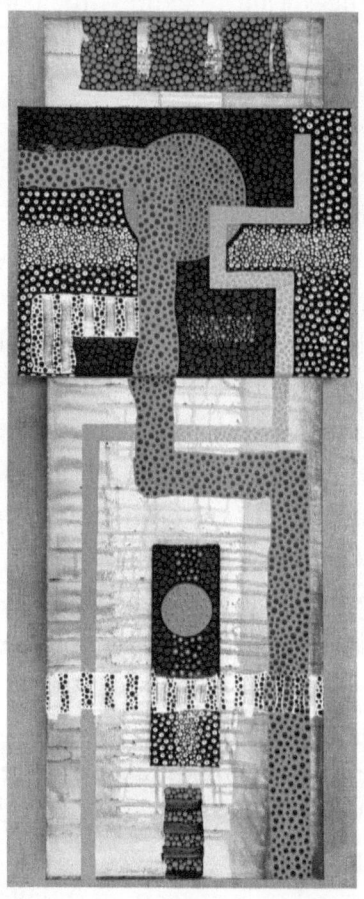

During quarantine, I have also observed how much of my mixed ethnic DNA reveals itself in what I create. Scientifically tracing my heritage not only to Italian, French, English, Irish and German ancestry, has also revealed ancient ties to Native American, Scandinavian, African and Middle Eastern peoples. While this scientific evidence supports my belief that, throughout the Earth, I am biologically connected, far more deeply than I often realize, it is through more intuitive experiences that I seek to interpret those connections.

So, how do I express those connections and the associated need for human contact during this time of great division, isolation, of distrust, and even blame? Having long used art as a language to express what I cannot speak with words, I have observed within myself a near uncontrollable urgency to interpret what is happening each day through the creative process. My artistic expression most often chooses to convey the universal, multi-layered experiences of humanity. However, during these many months of "dis-ease," my oeuvre is even more focused on tackling themes of restraint, fears and vulnerability born of the unknown, loss of income and business, racial protests compelled by a need to change centuries of systemic oppression, gender divides, and the necessity of swift adaptation to maintain emotional and mental health. While many of my go-to thematic elements – visible layers weaving in and out of those that are now covered; covertly-placed symbolism and typography that only reveal themselves with an interactive change in lighting and physical perspective; and vibrational color choices that invite the eye to move from places of abstract chaos to more calming sections of meditative intention - there is a palpable shift within my artistic expression being presently more informed by compression, constraint, isolation, and an empathetic longing to heal and plant "seeds" for a more equitable future for generations to come.

This longing has manifested itself even further into a series of work interpreting those critical, liminal points in one's life where the shock of events (most often outside one's personal sphere of life experience) create confusion, denial, and hopefully acceptance. These pivotal moments are most often followed by a compelling drive to seek verifiable truth and expanding awareness as to how oneself is connected to these truths. And then, lastly, there arrives an urgent need for action and a reboot of one's complacency, especially in regards to righting the wrongs of previous generations. Two recent pieces, "Liminal Divide" and "Liminal Divide II", contain within them furtive visual references to the blood of black brothers and sisters so often spilled by those in blue uniforms. The liminal divide is that point where privileged white populations are forced to confront their silent observations and move through a new, unexpected, and undeniably uncomfortable, rite of passage into vocal alliance and active protest. Painting what I often cannot put into words, this abstract series continues even deeper into interpretation of linear and non-linear aspects of human experience and memory, and how the experience and memories of one individual or group weave and layer themselves in close contact with the those of another.

Finally, and not surprisingly, many of my pandemic artworks have revealed themselves to be "accidental" talismans of sorts; reflecting a desire to have something, anything to hold onto (contact) during these rites of passage, into which to put our faith, dreams, and higher intentions. While struggling with my own responses to the external, uncontrollable "insanity" witnessed during current events, I found myself drawn, again and again, to express my responses through a filter/language of ancient, archetypal soul wisdom. Some of my painted responses are similar to cave paintings. Others feel like portals to another time and space. The most common thread through them all is that they contain within them an aura of talismanic "blessings"; one can exhibit in one's home or safe space as a way to invite good fortune during a time when our fortunes are swiftly rising and falling like the ocean tide. Do I have evidence of these talismanic blessings? Maybe so. While limited to my small home studio, I painted nearly 19 of these pieces and gratefully sold 9 of them during a time when people were losing their jobs and incomes and I was also forced to close my business. The funds from these art sales have made it possible for me to sustain my gallery/working studio space and remain a viable arts-centered business, supporting arts and culture in Las Vegas and beyond.

There is no doubt that these themes will continue to inform and guide my studio practice, my creative expression, and even my drive to serve my community. Until that time when we each choose to become living, breathing talismans for one another, i.e. blessing and supporting our fellow human beings, our talismans will remain objects into which we project that which our hearts and souls most desire.

Website: www.nancygoodart.com

Our Ever Changing World: Through the Eyes of Artists: Book 14

Debbi Swanson Patrick

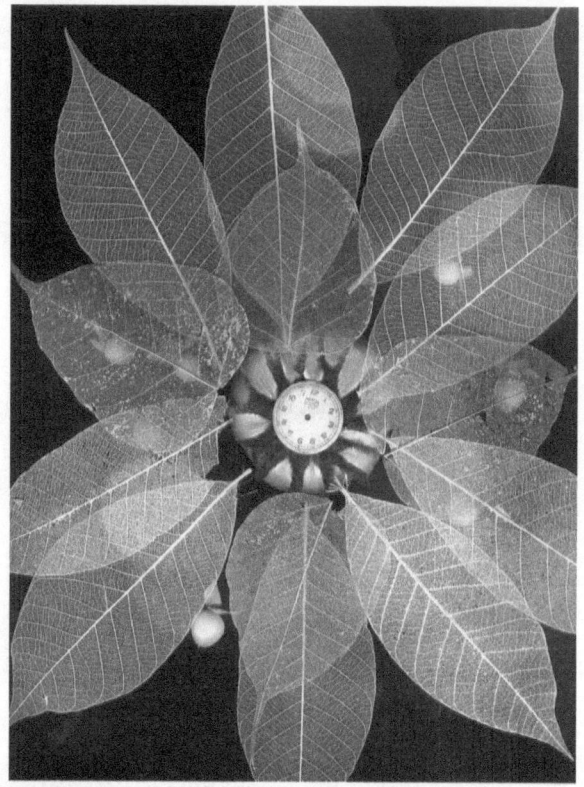

Name: Debbi Swanson Patrick
Discipline: Photography and Scanography
Country: United States of America

Pandemic + Art = Revelations
Pandemic + Art. For me they did not equal much in terms of creating art. This piece is my only completely finished work done in 2020 in my particular genre known as scanography. I call it digital still life. The title is Time to Reveal because this was a year when deep cracks

appeared in our country and relationships, and in a way, letting the light shine through.

I say that in a positive way, in spite of the damage, uncertainly, deaths, political insanity, and near destruction of our democracy perpetrated by an "unstable genius."

This is an opportunity to change our course, to move forward with compassion instead of egos, male dominance, idol worship, and short sightedness. Some people prefer the world is only about them. But I think we've seen, that will not work.

We dealt with many of the same challenges in 2020. Lockdowns, misinformation, shopping issues, masks/ gloves/ sanitizer, boredom, overwhelm, friends and loved ones lost by death or division.

We learned, it was revealed through this pandemic, that work doesn't have to be done in the same old ways. Crazy commutes can be modified or eliminated. Delivery services can meet some of our needs. Some business's creativity to stay alive were impressive. We are adaptable.

The future may look much different when COVID is over, or accepted as a new part of our lives and treated with boosters like the flu. When cracks appear, light gets in. Ideas change. Many of us had the chance to get off life's treadmill and ponder. Thank you to the dedicated frontline workers who made that possible.

With no studio photography work, early on I enjoyed the free time to get closer to neighbors, to ground myself in place. We would meet in the street for a little dance time, a chat, some laughs, a glass of wine sipped while slipping masks on and off quickly. We traded little gifts. I signed up for art workshops, photo classes and bought all kinds of new photo software tools. I have thousands of photographs to turn into presentable art.

And I did little. My brain couldn't go there. I wanted to, but I felt compelled to either reorganize my house, do other necessary tasks, or sleep. I had a lot of physical issues to contend with, and a lawsuit that I was waging over a dog attack in 2019 that caused some of them. I went in to have a pain control device surgically implanted in early March. There was too much scar tissue from previous surgeries on my back. In July a different approach was attempted and succeeded. I considered it my 65th birthday present.

For several months I was recovering as my body fused with the new device and the wires that lead from the battery placed near my hip, to my spine to interrupt the nerve communication and stop the pain. I got sort of used to the constant buzzing inside my body. Yes, I am the Bionic Woman. I have one artificial hip, my lower spine and three disks in my neck are fused. But while the Bionic

Woman could do anything with her techno body, mine is now more limited. But I'm here!

I also lacked creative and emotional space to work. People were at home, working here or just living. My boyfriend sold his house two days after listing it, in the middle of the Bobcat Fire, and his house was right near the fire line. It took several stressful weeks to get it cleaned up, decluttered, sold, then packed. Stuff ended up in my already full house.

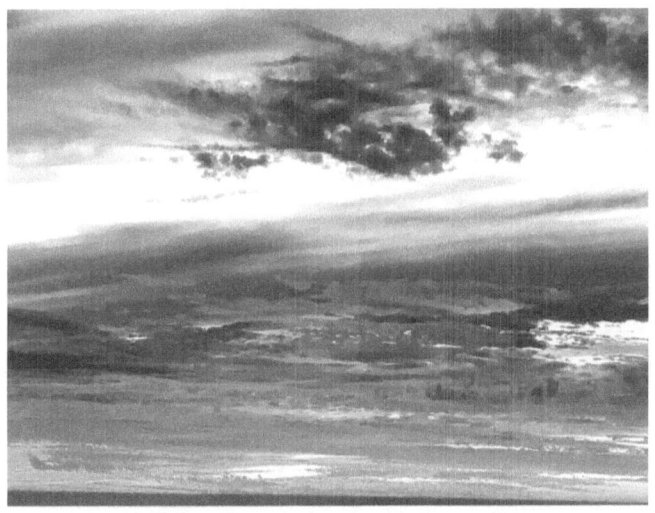

Here's the last sunset photo before the pandemic shutdown. Taken at sea on cruise to Mexico

Then I had to say goodbye to my sweet old lab Kirby, the dog who loved everybody. He was a bit of an Eyore, but so loving and sweet. His body just had dealt with too many weaknesses and he couldn't handle it anymore. I still hear him in the house. I recorded his wonderful blubbers when I rubbed his ears.

With my "me time," I listed to the Calm app. Several times a day. And napped. Like many, the underlying anxiety depleted me between bursts of energy. What I did do was create a miniature piece of art for my friend's "miniature farm house and art gallery show." And the tiny piece sold, as did many of the wonderful pieces in the show. I made new friends in our getaway place of Palm Springs by participating in Friday night Happy Hours led by an artist with an extraordinary personality. Themed bingo, name that tune, trivia, and costumes made up 90s minutes of semi-drunken loving hilarity. What a gift.

And as communications director for the Pasadena Society of Artists, I helped as several of us moved the group into the 21st century with online exhibitions and on-demand catalogs. We did three in six months, quite a feat for a volunteer organization that could only have zoom meetings. I continued to work with my business partner on a local magazine we produce. At times it felt impossible, yet it was a way for us to continue to connect to others. And it's paid off with new relationships and business.

So I hope this year, and always, space opens for all of us. In all kinds of new ways. And new opportunities are revealed. Blessings.

Website:
www.tellingimages.com
and www.debbiswanson.smugmug.com

Artist, ART, & Story: A Moment in Time, 2020: International

Ginger Van Hook

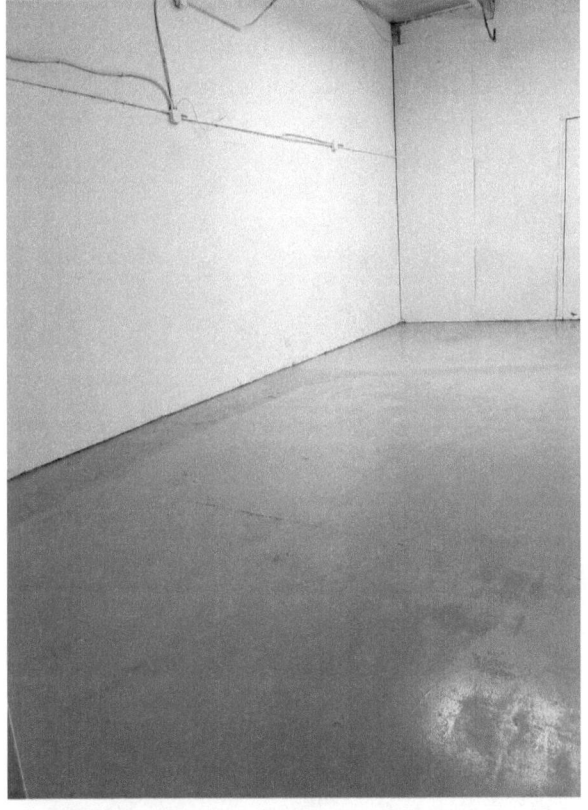

Name: Ginger Van Hook
Discipline: Photographer, Writer
Country: United States of America

What was I in the middle of doing when we were shut-down by the Virus?

I was arranging a space for exhibitions of art in the other building, next to my father's machine shop. I had engaged help from artists to help paint the walls and create a curatorial space for future exhibitions. We got as far as moving all the clutter to one side, painting the walls white, and the floors grey, then separating the contained beautiful pure white space expecting something great.

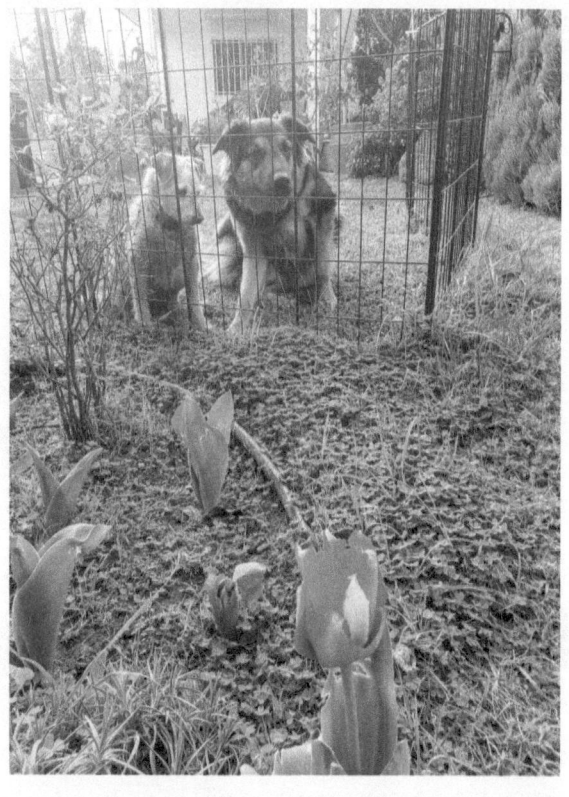

It was something great that happened alright; it was a great tragedy our planet experienced and at that moment I stood at the center of an empty space in March of 2020. Just a brief 12 months ago, my father, age 90, was alive. Just weeks ago it seems now, I was plotting which artists would be on the walls come that summer. But instead, at shutdown, not sundown, a great blank curatorial space became immediately filled with tables and a sewing machine. Next to that, a space for photographing products, artistically designed, all for Internet consumption. I delved into my father's world, cleaning his space and dusting off his relics. I had already made a small exhibition of my father's work in the front office. My father had been an inventor all his life, an artist at the core. I presumed I had some of his creative DNA so I put that into making masks to protect against the Corona Virus.

I photographed the product when it was completed, thus I utilized my photographic skills, from artist to marketer and engaged the assistance of valued artists who participated in my flights of fancy (…while we had otherwise nothing else to do?) But as an artist, was that not the best of all worlds? To be shutdown from having to work outside your creative space with no interruptions of social gatherings or polite conversation needed?

I seemed to thrive, and for following my father's precise instructions, I never shutdown the shop because in an instant, I realized his wisdom. We were essential workers. We still make things here inside America, with our hands, our hearts, our machines, our drive and our ambitions. As artists and artisans, we couldn't stop working or other folks would not get their medical or dental products, vehicles would not function without their bushings and space vehicles couldn't get off earth without their nuts and bolts. Essential workers saved lives every day, twenty-four hours a day, always including Sundays, Sad Days and Rainy Days. Thank you each and every one of you!

I continued to work, never dropping my pace, as I assumed, the virus was after me, and after my family. My mother was ill, so already with compromised immune issues, she was locked away at home and I evolved into caretaker; already familiar with this dedicated work as I had done it for my father. But I also delved into my own creativity as well. I carved out that big beautiful blank space and turned it into a functioning environment where even though at the time, the occupancy was a total of ONE, I knew, that eventually, by appointment, I could share ART, one by one to millions in the future.

We are now, one year later at the stages of re-opening. I am ready to face the new world; with or without a vaccine, I wear my designer masks. I am reaching out again to artists who wish to participate in my curatorial flights of fancy. We can show great art works locally and with luck, this can go viral in a super cool way. See you on the web. With love and hugs to you and all your loved ones, continue to work, that IS your job as an artist. No matter where, no matter what, just keep doing what you do because YOU are an ESSENTIAL HUMAN BEING.

Websites:
www.gingersartjournal.blogspot.com
www.finearttrekkinlosangeles.blogspot.com
www.gingervanhook.com
www.lukevanhook.com
www.ingelsengineeringservices.com

Artist, ART, & Story: A Moment in Time, 2020: International

Karrie Ross

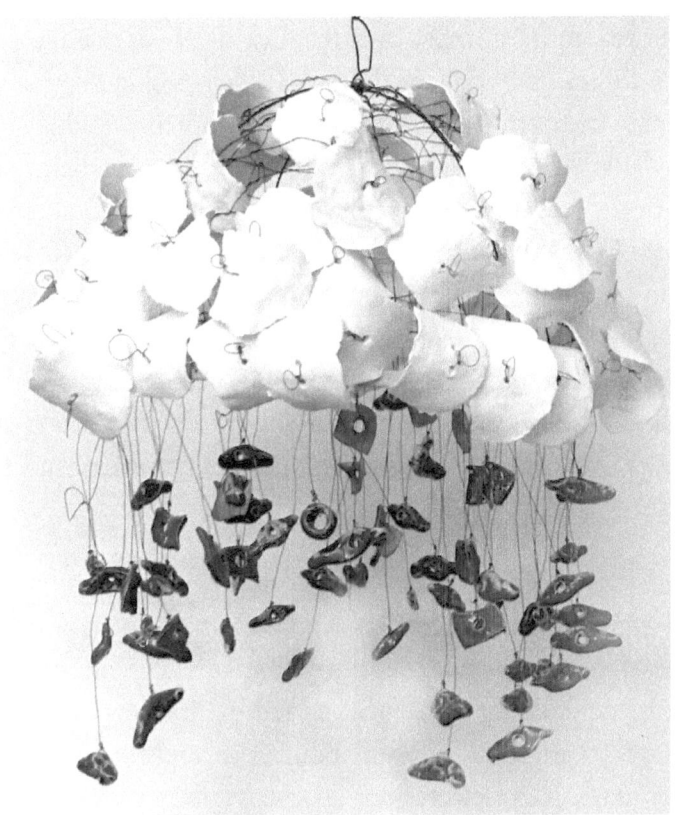

Name: Karrie Ross
Discipline: Visual Artist
Country: United States of America

2020:
The year started with another BANG! to my head, and a CT scan to be sure all is ok. I'm tired of this. I was in process of drawing a piece of art-a-day and my fall showed

up in the art.(see image at end of story) I didn't recognize it right off and when I did, I realized I needed to address how the fall was making me feel. By the time I did, it was already into February and the Covid-19 Pandemic was starting to take over the news and all ways of being that we knew up to that point. I kept drawing my images daily but by mid-April I started seeing dead people in them so I stopped the drawing. I found myself doing lots of internet searches for what to expect from the virus. Being 70 years old I became overly cautious. I immediately stopped meeting my friends and my ceramics class was cancelled. The endless seach for masks started and I couldn't find one that allowed me to breathe comfortably. Then the social fears began, the shortages on toilet paper and sanitizer and the fanatical thinking started...paranoia here it comes.

As the world began a "great change", art exhibitions became online exhibitions which opened up opportunities to show art outside of my immediate location and I was included in many unexpected exhibitions in out-of-state galleries and written about in several poetry books, art magazines, selected for special projects for museums, as well as several other online projects for artsits. So, at the beginning the fears of the art community coming to an end were unfounded as the whole of the artworld seemed to rise to the occasion to keep us all active and learning ... zoom became a 'norm' for all interactions and audiences grew as more sessions were opened up with discussions. I do not believe this will go away, the opportunity it allows us is great, to communicate and be part of a world community is endless.

Artist, ART, & Story: A Moment in Time, 2020: International

I don't usually watch the news but I started watching it now. The USA had the worst President of my life and at the time and most likely the history of our country. A sad example of a human being that lied more than he told the truth and with each word that came out of his mouth his manipulation was apparent... but there he was, telling us all that it, the virus, was 'nothing to worry about'. And in my opinion, he was right because in comparrison to him and the damage he did and was doing to our country the virus was "nothing to worry about' HE WAS the distruction of a whole system, a way of being and believing he... he was tearing it apart. Thank goodness our country came together in that belief and voted him out so the new President could worry about and start a process of fighting the virus, then begin to heal the damage that was done to our country.

I live with my son and he was now home everyday working from home which was driving him crazy. So I took to creating projects for me, for him to help me with and eventually things started to take on a new flavor and his work opened up to two or three half days a week he went in to keep the labs going.

Then in July I found out that my friend Roger passed away in his sleep. We had just started an on-going conversation and were laughing and being creative. His death rocked the wall I had put up to keep out the horror that was going on outside "my life", I cried, sobbed for quite the while, he was a good person, a creative artist/photographer. A man who gave freely and opened my perspective for the better. I miss him and will think and remember him and his words always.

One of the projects I created for my son and I was we bought a car, a 2002 Mercury Grand Marquis which he immediately started fixing up so I could drive it, but I knew I wouldn't be able to but did not tell him, he was having such a good time finding all the parts to make it "better" and he was totally occupied. Whew!

Towards the end of the year, October, I found a ceramics studio to fire and glaze at which helped me get things going again. I was having so much fun learning the differences that the studio had from my last one. I moved forward slowly. By the end of November I was firering every week and started making several of my winged ballerina and angels. Creativity seemed to come home.

I was contacted to be a part of a unique online exhibition at Suturo with a new mobile-like piece "Dandelions in Flight"; 20x18x18, www.suturo.com. (see image at beginning of the story). I was happy to be asked.

Eventually my son and I took the Mercury for a ride on Route 39, a nice winding road into the mountains. During the ride my eyes got wonky and my body started to react to the too-soft seat and general ride. This started me on the path to a really bad case of vertigo that reslulted in sciatica that took me out completely. I could not think and lost four book design jobs at the end of the year. This illness and all the effects lasted for 4-plus months.

Artist, ART, & Story: A Moment in Time, 2020: International

January 1st, 2021 was about the time my son started being quarantined, which of course meant I was too, but due to circumstances beyond my control my quarantine lasted almost a month and stopped me from getting any help i could get for the sciatica... anyways... thankful to be here I signed up for my first vaccine Pfizer, end of February with the second in March.

This is a selective recounting of the year I experience, not really any specific moment, but the whole year was a "moment in time" of change and deep reflection. Everything revolved around the coronavirus, quarantine pandemic and making the USA and world safe again.

Website: www.karrieross.com
www.artistartandstory.com

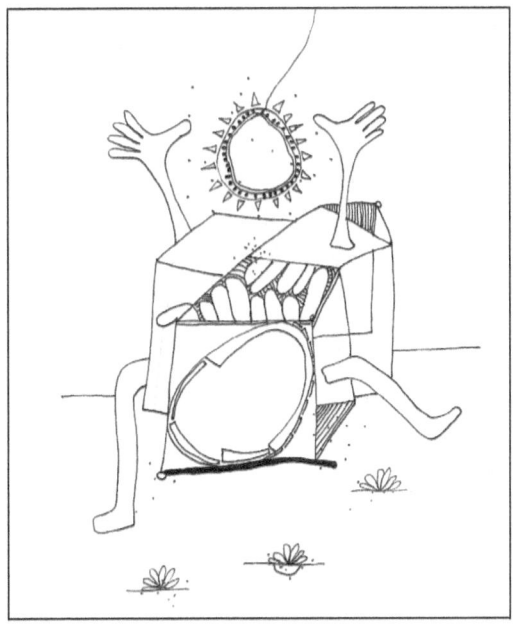

The fall.

Our Ever Changing World: Through the Eyes of Artists: Book 14

Roger Morrison
He is remembered. July 25, 2020

Karrie Ross is with **Roger Morrison**.
July 25, 2020

072520 My dear friend Roger Morrison left this world last week peacefully in his sleep. Years ago he showed up one day at my space at the Beverly Hills show and we've been friends ever since. I loved his love of art and humor, he made me laugh. One of the most kind, generous, thoughtful people ever. He is remembered 🖤 with lots of love. This is a photo of him and a photo of his from Memorial Day, a beautiful honor to his fellow Veterans and our Flag. 🖤🖤

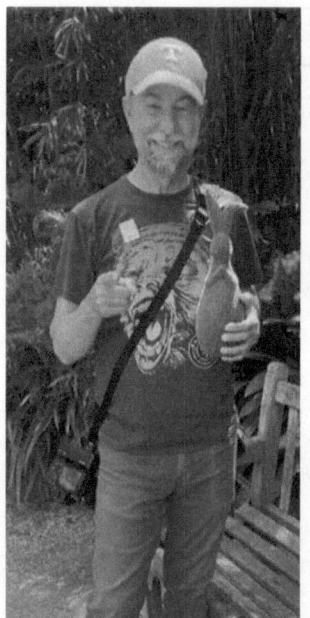

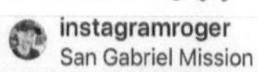
instagramroger
San Gabriel Mission

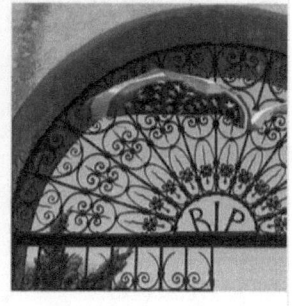

Liked by **joe_fay_artis** others

instagramroger "The Flag Eagle" © ROGERtheArtist this Memorial Day 2020, l(

Name: Roger Morrison
Discipline: Photograher
Country: United States of America

Artist, ART, & Story: A Moment in Time, 2020: International

Roland Reiss
He is remembered. December 13, 2020

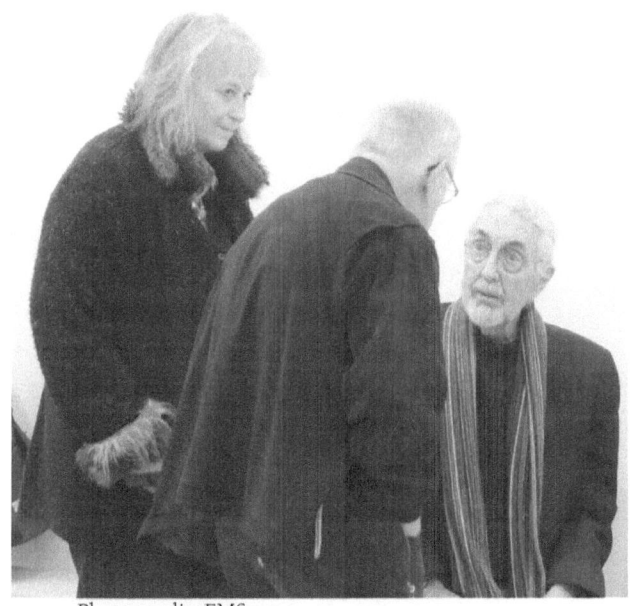

Photo credit: EMS

Name: Roland Reiss
Discipline: Artist, painter, teacher
Country: United States of America
https://www.legacy.com/obituaries/dailycamera/obituary.aspx?n=roland-reiss&pid=198033917&utm_source=facebook&utm_medium=social&utm_campaign=obitshareamp&utm_content=p198033917&fbclid=IwAR0vtLVCxNLmDiZ_SPTE4_dqYRnWz8oB9I2JO4P0jDWGoJsCzPCTSbqzoyw

Our Ever Changing World:
Through the Eyes of Artists

Artist Art & Story
A Moment in Time, 2020
International

Please join us for
Book #15
soon to come.

www.ingramcontent.com/pod-product-compliance
Lightning Source LLC
Chambersburg PA
CBHW031615210526
45464CB00004B/1590